All-Color Guide

Dogs

Selection • Care • Training

by Wendy Boorer

Illustrated by Edward Osmond

Bantam Books
Toronto • New York • London

FOREWORD

This book covers all aspects of care for the dog owner. Advice is given on the choice and rearing of a pet puppy, followed by a short section on the dog's senses and canine behavior in general. The basics of training are given in detail, whether for the pet or the show dog. The techniques of coat trimming will help the dog owner who becomes interested in the show ring, while the pages on breeding show stock and kennel management assist those who are fascinated by the dog game. A knowledge of genetics for the layman and a brief account of inherited abnormalities in the dog will give the kennel owner some clues in evolving a breeding program. The section on anatomy concentrates on the relationship of structure to conformation and movement, and this is followed by a section covering ways of recognizing ill-health. The comprehensive glossary explains many of the terms and abbreviations unfamiliar to those who are new to the world of dogs.

DOGS: SELECTION, CARE, TRAINING
A Bantam Book / published by arrangement with
Grosset & Dunlap, Inc.
PRINTING HISTORY
Grosset & Dunlap All-Color Guide hardcover edition
published February 1971
Bantam edition / May 1972
6 printings through September 1978

Bantam Books are published by Bantam Books, inc. Its trademark, consisting of the words "Bantam Books" and the portrayal of a bantam, is registered in the United States Patent Office and in other countries. Marca Registrada. Bantam Books, Inc., 666 Fifth Avenue, New York, New York 10019.

0 9 8 7 6

CONTENTS

4   **Choosing and Buying a Dog**

10   **Looking After Your Dog**
10   The puppy
18   The adult dog
24   The old dog

28   **The Dog's Senses**

34   **Dog Behavior**

44   **Training**
47   Domestic training
54   Specialized training

74   **Showing Dogs**

96   **Breeding Dogs**

122   **Kennel Management**

134   **Anatomy**

147   **Ill Health**

154   **Glossary**

158   **Index**

CHOOSING AND BUYING A DOG

The companionship of a dog gives pleasure to millions of people, and the choice of an animal, which can become a loved member of the family, deserves more thought than it often receives. The haphazard acquisition of a puppy may bring unexpected joy into a home, but too often, it brings problems as well, which a little forethought might have avoided. The responsibilities of dog ownership are sometimes forgotten, and those who have no time to exercise their pet, or who are likely to be absent for long periods of every day, would do better to choose some less demanding animal.

There is a lot to be said for having a pedigreed animal in whose appearance the owner can take pride. All puppies are fun, but the mongrel may well end up a larger, hairier and indeed uglier animal than its appearance as a pup might lead

one to suspect. With a purebred puppy this gamble can be avoided. There are over 350 breeds of dog in the world so the choice is extremely wide. One of the best methods of seeing what breeds are available is to visit a large dog show. There are also a number of books on the market with photographs of all the breeds, and these can be a great help.

If you feel like giving a home to a stray which might otherwise be destroyed, you can at least be sure it is healthy if you get it from one of the accredited animal homes.

Unless the breed of dog is being chosen for a specific purpose, such as a guard dog or a gundog, the following general

5

points should be taken into account. The breed of your choice should be one you can afford to feed, house and exercise. Although this seems obvious, too many dogs are given away when they are adult because they grew too large. A long-coated breed will need more time spent on coat care to preserve that glamorous look. Some breeds have less doggy odor than others and some shed hair less. There are temperamental differences between breeds as well, although these are not so clearly definable as the physical differences. Although a dog's behavior is very much influenced by its upbringing, some breeds tend to be more phlegmatic than others, some noisier, some more affectionate and others naturally protective.

Whether to have a dog or a bitch also needs consideration. Males tend to be larger, bolder and more independent. Bitches come into season twice a year and have to be kept away from male dogs during these periods if mating is to be prevented. They are less likely to roam.

Most people start with a puppy, but it should not be forgotten that if an adult is preferred, many breeders have surplus stock which will make very satisfactory pets. A number of commercial establishments specialize in providing pedigreed puppies, and a good firm will sell puppies already wormed and inoculated, with a veterinary certificate of health and sometimes a guarantee for a specific time period. The price will normally be higher than a comparable puppy of equal quality bought direct from a breeder.

The most satisfactory way of buying is to find a kennel specializing in the breed you want. Here puppies are more likely to have received individual attention and less likely to have met infection. If you are interested in one of the lesser known breeds this will probably be the only way of finding a puppy. Dog

Greyhound racing

magazines carry advertisements under breed headings. Alternatively most breeds have clubs catering for their interests. In all countries where pedigreed dogs are valued, there is a Kennel Club which will be able to supply the name and address of the breed club secretary, who, in turn, will help you to find the nearest kennels.

Puppies are usually sold no younger than eight weeks old. Younger than this they can still be successfully reared but are going to need extra care and attention. For a novice choosing a pet puppy, good health and good temperament are the things to look for. A healthy puppy is lively, has a well-rounded appearance, loose, supple skin and no discharge from the eyes or nose. If the litter is being kept under filthy conditions or any of the puppies are listless, do not buy. Temperament is more difficult to judge, particularly as the temperament of an adult dog depends a great deal on the handling that it has received. A nervous bitch usually means nervous pups. Picking the boldest and naughtiest pup quite often means you are getting the most intelligent — and also the one most likely to need and respond best to training. With your purchase you should get a copy of the pedigree, a registration application form showing that the litter has been registered with the American Kennel Club, and a transfer form signed by the breeder so that the dog's new ownership will be recorded. A diet sheet and inoculation details should also be supplied.

Try to avoid the shy puppy
which does not want to make friends.

Temperamental differences show
early.

LOOKING AFTER YOUR DOG

The puppy

Introducing a puppy to a new home and family should be done in a calm and relaxed way. The puppy may well appear apprehensive in strange surroundings, and it should be allowed to explore in its own time. Many people worry about introducing a new puppy into a household containing other pets. Usually such worries are groundless provided the causes of jealousy are kept to a minimum.

Puppies should always be handled gently and spoken to quietly, as it is essential they should have confidence in their owner before they can be taught anything. Never pick a dog up suddenly or roughly. Always support the animal's body weight with your arm and hold firmly without clutching. A bitch will carry her pups by the scruff of their necks, but by eight weeks old most puppies are too heavy to be carried in this fashion.

Every dog should have its own bed in a warm, quiet, draft-

The bitch will carry young puppies like this.

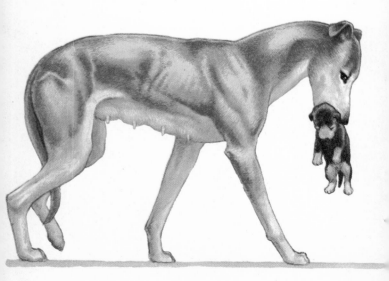

free place. Puppies are destructive, so elaborate and expensive equipment should not be used. A stout cardboard box placed on its side makes a good bed for a puppy which is going to live indoors, as it is easily replaced when it falls to pieces or is outgrown. Bedding should be easily washable and easily replaceable. Cast-off clothing with the buttons and zippers removed or old towels are a sensible choice. It is very useful too, in the early stages, to have a puppy pen. It should be lightweight for use both indoors and out.

The puppy should always be supported underneath.

Your new puppy should be made to feel as secure as possible.

It is a good plan if possible to bring home a new puppy early in the day. After a day spent exploring the sights and smells of a new home, the puppy may be tired enough to sleep through the night without fuss. Most puppies however, finding themselves alone for the first time, yelp or howl during the night. This should be ignored if at all possible and, after two or three nights, most dogs will have become accustomed to the new situation. It is not kind or logical to punish a puppy for being distressed during its first nights away from the litter. Try to make sure the puppy has a good romp in the evening and is tired at bedtime. A well-wrapped, hot-water bottle will give it something warm to snuggle up to, and sometimes a loudly ticking clock nearby will work like a charm in convincing the puppy that it has not been entirely abandoned.

Young puppies, like babies, need plenty of attention, lots of uninterrupted sleep and frequent feeding. If your puppy came with a diet sheet, follow it, and if you wish to introduce changes do so gradually. A general rule is to give four meals a day from eight weeks to three months old, three meals a day from three to six months, and two meals a day from six months to a year. An adult need only be fed once a day, though many people still prefer to give a morning and evening meal. The dog's main food is meat, and in the case of puppies, two meals should be meat and two milk, thickened with some sort of cereal. The meat will have to be cut up or minced to start with, and whether it is fed raw or cooked is immaterial. If cooked meat is used the gravy should also be fed. The type of meat can be varied. During the teething stage a large shank bone is helpful. Make certain the bones are not sharp and do not splinter. Cheese, eggs and boneless fish can be used in moderation instead of meat. The milk meals can consist of puppy meal soaked in milk, and it is a good idea to add some form of mineral and vitamin supplement to ensure the diet is adequate for growth.

Make sure the puppy is safe
when left on its own.

Puppies have an instinct to keep their bed clean, and as soon as they can move about they will stagger away from the nest before relieving themselves. An eight-week-old puppy has not got a great deal of control over bladder and bowel movements, and the length of time taken for housetraining depends a lot on the owner's vigilance. Puppies cannot wait and will need to go out as soon as they wake up, after each meal and after any energetic romp. They will need to relieve themselves at least seven or eight times a day and cannot be expected to be clean and dry throughout the night. For this reason it is usually helpful to train the puppy to use newspaper. Newspaper should be spread on the floor and the puppy watched carefully. As soon as it shows signs of wanting to squat, it should be rushed to the newspaper and praised if it relieves itself there. All mistakes indoors should be cleaned up very thoroughly, as the smell of that spot will act as a reminder to the puppy, which will tend to use the same place again. It is now possible to buy a liquid, the smell of a few drops of which on a newspaper will attract a puppy

The results of some American research suggest that lead training is significantly easier at the fifth, seventh and ninth weeks of age.

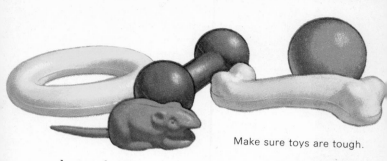

Make sure toys are tough.

toward using the same spot. Quicker results will be obtained by a watchful owner prepared to praise the right action, than by one who merely scolds mistakes.

Puppies get enough exercise by playing but should be accustomed to a collar and lead at an early age. Even if you do not intend your dog to wear a collar all the time, start by buckling a light collar round the puppy's neck and leaving it there for several days until its presence is ignored. The collar should be just tight enough so that it cannot be slipped over the head.

Do not let your dog pull.

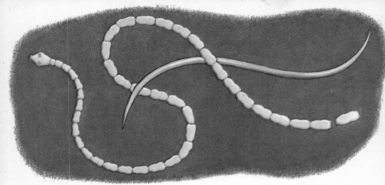
Tapeworms are segmented. Roundworms are excreted whole.

All puppies should be inoculated against distemper before being allowed to meet any strange dogs or being allowed to walk on ground to which other dogs have access. Also included in the immunization should be protection against hepatitis, a severe virus disease which attacks the liver, and two forms of Leptospiral infections. The inoculations take the form of injections which are usually given at three months old, but may be given earlier. Your veterinary surgeon will advise the right time and will also recommend booster inoculations when these become necessary. In the United States, as well as in some other countries where rabies is present, anti-rabies inoculations can be given at six months of age.

The dog has a number of internal parasites, the one most common in puppies being the roundworm. This looks like a dirty, yellowish piece of string, being anything from two to eight inches in length, with slightly pointed ends. The larvae of the roundworm can migrate through the bloodstream of a pregnant bitch to the embryonic puppies, who may thus be infected with worms at birth. A puppy from a reputable source will have been wormed before sale, but if your puppy was not, it should be taken to a veterinary surgeon who will prescribe tablets. Alternatively roundworm pills can be bought at many drug and pet stores and, provided the puppy is otherwise healthy and the instructions on the packet are followed carefully, the animal can be treated at home. Cleanliness of the dog's surroundings helps prevent reinfection, and all infected feces should be burned. Many dog breeders worm puppies first at six weeks and again around four months.

The changes and growth achieved during the first year obviously depend a great deal on the type of dog. However, the following generalities can be made. Up to twelve weeks puppies spend a great deal of time exploring their surroundings by which time they have virtually achieved complete independence. From three to four months they begin to lose their rotund appearance and become leggy. At about four months the milk teeth begin to fall out, and the adult teeth come through. From six to eight months the proportions of the body often lengthen, and the puppy fluff of a long-haired dog starts being replaced, although in many cases the full adult coat will not be achieved until two to three years. From six months to the end of the growth period the food intake will be greater than that of an adult.

Healthy puppies love to play.

17

The adult dog

While the care of a healthy, adult dog should be largely a matter of common sense, some special tips for special dogs may be useful. If you own a very large breed, bear in mind that such animals mature late and continue to need mineral, calcium and phosphorus supplements at least until the dog is two years old or more. All large dogs should be fed off the ground if possible, as this encourages the proper stance and good straight bone. Large, heavy breeds like St. Bernards will not need the amount of exercise that their size might suggest. Training for large, active dogs, such as Great Danes, should start early, as by six months they are already too large to handle easily. If you should be tempted to breed a litter from your bitch, remember that large breeds often have litters to match and rearing a dozen giants may not be an economical proposition.

Small dogs have many of the opposite characteristics, maturing early and having small litters. Some are delicate and need protection against extremes of cold and heat. Because of miniaturization the teeth of toy dogs are often very

A feeding bench helps large dogs maintain a good front stance and helps prevent splayed legs.

Simple shelters for dogs that are only penned for short periods.

crowded in the jaw, and care of the teeth is most important. Nails, too, are likely to need attention, as such small dogs are not able to wear them down sufficiently by exercise. Special clippers must be used, as scissors are useless, and it is important to remember that the nail has a living quick growing inside it, and if this is cut, it is extremely painful to the dog.

The care of the dog should be the responsibility of one member of the family who can maintain regularity in feeding, grooming, watering and exercising. Dogs are very much creatures of habit, and a routine helps the owner to make sure that nothing has been forgotten. No dog should be allowed to roam. Country dogs are likely to get into trouble chasing stock, and all dogs are liable to be involved in road accidents. When there is no one to give it individual attention, a dog should either be shut indoors or in a pen with some protection against the weather. If the dog is only penned for short periods of the day, this protection need not be elaborate. It should provide shade, shelter from wind and rain, and somewhere to lie off wet ground.

The dog has the teeth and digestion of a carnivore and therefore the main ingredient of its diet should be meat.

19

Meat can be fed raw or cooked, and if it is cooked the gravy should also be fed, as this will contain some of the minerals. If the meat is raw and frozen it should not be fed until it has thoroughly thawed. The idea that a dog should not be given fat is a mistaken one. Provided that the proportion is kept to a reasonable level, fat is beneficial. Chopped meat should not be left in the air for long periods as it goes stale very quickly and loses its vitamin content. Fat, cheese, eggs and fish are all good in moderation, though the fish must be boned and pressure cooked and should not be given more than once a week. A wild carnivore, having made a kill, eats the paunch and intestines of the victim first. The partially digested vegetable matter in the stomach provides vitamins and trace elements which would otherwise be missing from an all-meat diet. These trace elements can be fed to the domestic dog in the form of mineral and vitamin supplements

Diagram of approximate food intake to weight ratio

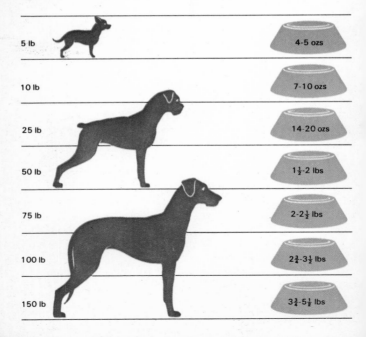

5 lb	4-5 ozs
10 lb	7-10 ozs
25 lb	14-20 ozs
50 lb	$1\frac{1}{2}$-2 lbs
75 lb	2-$2\frac{1}{2}$ lbs
100 lb	$2\frac{3}{4}$-$3\frac{1}{2}$ lbs
150 lb	$3\frac{3}{4}$-$5\frac{1}{2}$ lbs

to the diet. The over-use of such supplements can be harmful, so follow the directions. If two-thirds of the diet is protein such as meat, the rest can be made up of table scraps or the largest dog biscuits that your dog is prepared to tackle. Canned dog foods are extremely convenient, but they are an expensive way of feeding an animal. In the United States the law requires the constituents of a pet food to be printed on the label, so you can be sure of exactly what you are getting.

The amount of food a dog needs can only be decided on a trial-and-error basis, as this varies so much with each individual. A working dog may need up to four times the amount of food necessary for a sedentary pet. Growing puppies, pregnant and nursing bitches all need extra amounts of regular food as well as bone-building supplements. The best way to judge is to notice how the dog's weight is on the amount of food it is getting.

Exercise should be a daily must, with all but the smallest dogs getting an hour or so, part of which should be galloping off the lead. Lethargic dogs should be encouraged to play retrieving ball games, which give the maximum of exercise to the dog with the minimum of effort for the owner.

If used, coat should cover the chest and abdomen.

21

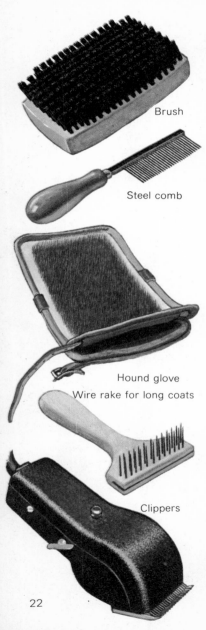

Brush

Steel comb

Hound glove

Wire rake for long coats

Clippers

A smooth-haired dog is best groomed with a hound glove, and a final shine can be obtained by polishing with a piece of silk or velvet. Wire-haired dogs and those with slightly longer coats need a short-bristled brush and a medium-sized steel comb. As well as brushes, a wide-toothed comb is useful for long-haired breeds. All dogs should, if possible, be groomed on a bench or table. Special attention should be paid to the areas behind the ears, inside the elbows, under the stomach, inside the thighs and between the toes, as mats tend to form in all these places.

A well-groomed dog will rarely need a bath, and puppies and older dogs are better off not bathed at all. A dog which enjoys rolling and comes home smelling badly will often be found to have only a small area of fur soiled, and this can be sponged clean. Tomato puree is a good deodorant for emergency use. Cleansing powders, which are rubbed into the coat and then brushed out, and aerosol shampoos are both easier, though slightly less effective, than a full-scale bath. A well wrung out chamois leather will absorb a lot of mud or, alternatively, newspaper can be used to dry a wet and muddy animal.

If your dog is of a breed that requires trimming or clipping, you can either have it done professionally at regular intervals, or learn to do it yourself. A demonstration by an expert will teach you a great deal. A photograph of a well-trimmed show specimen is also a good guide. If you are merely trimming a pet terrier, you can use a special stripping knife to take off the old coat. If you are preparing the dog for showing, the slower method of plucking out the hair between the finger and thumb gives a better finished look.

If fleas are suspected, the dog should be dusted with an insect powder recommended for animal use. Various kinds of lice will attach themselves to dogs. Before pulling them off a dab of methylated spirits or eau de cologne will persuade them to loosen their hold, otherwise a sore spot is likely. Ears and teeth should be checked periodically to see that they are clean. A dog that takes plenty of exercise will keep its own nails short, but the dew

Nail clippers

Flea

Louse

Chihuahua

claws should be watched as sometimes these get torn or grow around in a complete circle into the flesh. Over-long nails can be cut shorter with clippers, being very careful to avoid the quick.

The old dog
As a dog gets older it appreciates warmth and comfort more and is less able to withstand wet and cold. Its exercise should

Papillon

be taken at a slower pace, and it should be carefully dried after a wet outing. Many old dogs appreciate a coat in cold weather, and it should be one that protects the chest and stomach as well as the back. Old dogs which are going deaf should not be shouted at but shown what to do by touch or sign. Those with failing sight often have little difficulty in adapting to this. Most old dogs resent the rough play of younger animals and should not be expected to enjoy romping with children or puppies. In fact they should generally be allowed to take life at their own pace.

The regularity of feeding time becomes increasingly important to an aging animal. Many old dogs are too fat, but any dieting must be done very slowly as all sudden changes should be avoided. Extra vitamins are beneficial and food should be cut up small for a dog whose teeth are not in a very good state.

It is more important than ever that an old dog has a warm, dry, draft-proof bed. It should be one that it can get into easily and should be large enough for it to lie out flat, as the dog may be too stiff to curl up comfortably. Some old dogs can no longer last the night without emptying their bladder. Newspaper spread near the bed will help the cleaning up.

However clean they are kept, old animals smell more

Shih Tzu

Border Terrier

strongly. If you are certain the smell does not come from bad teeth, dirty ears or blocked anal glands, then daily chlorophyll tablets will remove the worst of the odor. There has recently been marketed a rejuvenating drug for dogs. This is given in tablet form daily. It in no way lengthens the dog's life but does remove some of the effects of old age and so enables it to get more enjoyment out of its last years.

Possibly the greatest sadness in owning a dog is the shortness of its life when compared with our own.

Samoyed

Though the decision to end the life of a family dog can be a hard and painful one to make, modern techniques ensure an ending both swift and painless. A very strong sedative an hour or two before will prevent the dog even feeling apprehension at the visit of the veterinary surgeon.

In general the largest breeds have the shortest lives, and many very big dogs are starting to age at seven or eight years of age. Toy breeds (though not the very tiniest individuals) and small terriers are quite often fit and spry at the age of twelve. Generalizations on longevity are misleading, but it would seem more sensible to choose a breed whose appearance is free from exaggeration. Evidence suggests, too, that dogs that are worked regularly, remain physically and mentally active longer than fireside pets. It is not that unusual for a dog to reach seventeen years of age, and a few individuals have lived more than twenty years. Longevity records are notoriously difficult to prove, but there are recent, well-authenticated cases of a Border Terrier, a Samoyed and a Curly-coated Retriever, all living for more than twenty years.

Curly-coated Retriever

THE DOG'S SENSES

To understand a little of the world as seen by the dog, it is useful to compare the dog's senses with our own. It is obvious that the dog relies a good deal less on sight than we do. Most dogs adapt to blindness remarkably well. Blind dogs will continue to retrieve balls, apparently locating them by sound and smell, and it has been known for a blind sheep-dog, which lost its sight after training, to work sheep successfully.

The structure of a dog's eye gives us some idea of the limitations of its sight. There is no evidence for color vision in any mammals except men, monkeys and apes, so the dog is color blind. Dogs do not possess the especially sensitive patch on the retina of the eye which gives us our acute vision. A dog is unable to move its eyes freely in their sockets, and this, together with the fact that in many breeds the eyes are positioned at the sides of the head, means a loss of stereoscopic, binocular vision. The dog compensates for this by having a longer, more mobile neck and by turning its head more frequently than we do. The exceptions to this are the

A dog has a considerably shorter line of vision than a person does.

Gazehounds use sight more than scent for hunting.

flat-faced breeds, such as the Pekinese and the Pug, where the position of the eyes at the front of the skull enable them to have some binocular vision.

It is very often forgotten by the average owner how much the dog's field of vision is governed by the animal's size. The horizon must be very near for a dog whose head is only a foot from the ground. This applies even more strongly to a dog that is swimming. Unless it can lift its head well above the water in order to look around, the amount a swimming dog can see must be restricted to a few feet.

Some breeds have inherited eye defects, and those with protruding eyes are more prone to eye damage and ulceration; otherwise differing eye sizes and shapes appear to have little effect on the ability to see. Though in most breeds a dark eye is preferred, there is no evidence to suggest that the coloring of the iris has any effect on the function of the eye. The dog with the partially pigmented wall-eye can see just as well.

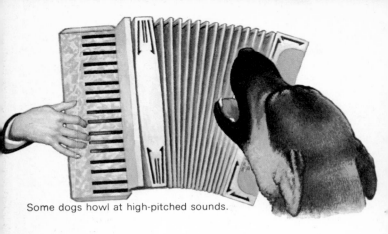
Some dogs howl at high-pitched sounds.

Dogs bred to hunt their quarry by sight are credited with the sharpest vision. Movement is undoubtedly what attracts and holds a dog's attention to something in the distance, which normally it would ignore.

Very little has been published about a dog's sense of taste, though dog food manufacturers have done a good deal of research in order to improve the palatability of their product. As the sense of smell and the sense of taste are so closely related and the former is so sensitive in the dog, it is not surprising to find that dogs can identify a particular flavor with 97.8 percent accuracy.

The 'silent' dog whistle takes advantage of the fact that dogs can hear a much higher range of sound than their owners. When such a whistle is blown, it emits a sound so shrill that it is inaudible to humans but perfectly audible to a dog. Adult humans respond to a range of sounds between 20 and 20,000 cycles per second, while children may hear sounds up to 40,000 or 50,000 cycles per second. The dog, however, hears 80,000 to 90,000 cycles per second, and in addition has a much greater capacity to distinguish the intensity and character of sounds. This is easily illustrated by the pet dog that will pick out the sound of the family car before the human ear detects any sound at all, or by the guard dog that not only hears a movement long before its owner, but can also decide whether it is made by friend or foe. A dog can distinguish the intervals between sounds of about one-fortieth of a second.

This sensitivity of hearing accounts for the number of sound-shy dogs there are. In many cases familiarity with the frightening sound will bring indifference to it, but in other cases this fear is an inherited trait that no amount of training will remove. It would be logical to suppose that dogs with pendent ears, or narrow, hair-filled ear canals, should not be able to hear as well as the prick-eared varieties, but in practice the difference is not discernible.

Another sense that is important in some specialized dog training fields, is what can be called contact sense or body sensitivity. A dog with low body sensitivity will shoulder its way through obstacles, while one with

Dogs used for guiding the blind wear special harnesses.

31

high body sensitivity will weave about, preferring to preserve a distance between itself and surrounding objects. This is taken into account when a dog is selected for training as a guide for the blind. Dogs with high body sensitivity are unsuitable as in their efforts to avoid obstacles they would ignore their master's needs.

Whereas humans rely mainly on sight, the most important sense to a dog is the sense of smell. The portion of the brain concerned with olfaction is correspondingly larger in the dog, and it is obvious when watching dog behavior that scent signals are most important.

When we look at the anatomy of a dog's nose we see that the nasal cavity is divided throughout with a partition of bone, in effect giving the dog two noses just as it has two eyes or two ears. As two ears help the dog to judge the direction of a sound, so two nasal chambers help the dog to judge the source of an odor. Each nasal cavity extends from the nostril through the upper jaw as far back as the eyeball. It is divided into many compartments by spongy bones,

Bloodhound

massive looking but really exceedingly light and delicate, being filled with air cavities separated by parchment-like partitions. These bones regulate the flow of air and are covered by the olfactory membrane. This membrane is immense, not only covering all the interstices and convolutions of the spongy bones, but also being wrinkled in on itself. It has been calculated that the area of this membrane is as large as the skin covering the body of the dog.

When a dog is scenting, not only does it sniff the air, ensuring a greater flow of air throughout the entire nasal chamber, it also produces much more saliva, so that the minute, scent-bearing particles are picked up and savored by the tongue as well as reaching the olfactory membrane, which, in turn, is connected to the brain by a very plentiful olfactory nerve supply. When a dog is tracking, its temperature rises, and it may concentrate so much on the information received through its nose that it may literally fall over the object of its search before its eyes appear to register it.

European Customs use dogs to search for drugs.

33

Dog guarding its home ground.

DOG BEHAVIOR

Most dog behavior is instinctive and can be paralleled by similar behavior in the wild dog species. Some knowledge of basic behavior patterns is desirable before we attempt to modify them by experience, training or environment.

As is to be expected in an animal that relies a great deal on its nose, marking by scent forms a very important part of dog behavior. This is most noticeable with the frequent urination of the male. This leg-lifting posture normally appears at about 19 weeks, and the frequency of urination follows a set pattern while the dog is in familiar surroundings and situations. The quantity of urine need only be a few drops which are placed high up to be more noticeable, and male dogs hardly ever completely empty their bladder. Bitches also urinate, for the same reason, less compulsively than males, but increasing in frequency just before they

come into season. The vigorous scratching up of the earth after defecation fulfills the same scent-marking function.

It has been stated that scent-marking evolved from elimination caused by fear, into a ritual used to familiarize and reassure an animal in a strange environment. It may be partly this that causes an otherwise house-trained dog to lift its leg in each room of a new home. Scent-marking has other functions as well, being often a statement of proprietary interest either in territory that the dog thinks belongs to it, or in a member of the opposite sex.

Dogs have an innate territorial impulse which man has always made use of to guard his home and belongings. In the wild, a pack of dogs will defend their territory, and a bitch will defend her den. Aggression in the domestic dog seems to be increased by tying it up for long periods, presumably because the chain effectively cuts off the dog's line of retreat and attack is the only defense left.

Bitch in season being pursued by suitors.

Sexual behavior among wild dogs, and domestic dogs that live in complete freedom, follows the same general pattern. The pro-estrus period, when the bitch becomes sexually attractive though ovulation has not yet occurred, is characterized by a swollen vulva and a blood-stained discharge. The bitch urinates more frequently. Her anal glands also secrete an attractive odor, and this helps to draw the attention of males. Throughout this courtship period, the bitch will be followed continuously by a varying number of dogs who will fight among themselves for precedence. The bitch will, at this stage, drive them off. This pro-estrus stage usually lasts about eleven days in the domestic dog. When estrus occurs and the bitch is ready to be mated, she will stand for the male in a characteristic pose with the tail twisted to one side and the swollen vulva exposed. This period of receptivity varies in length in the domestic dog, being usually from two to five days. During this time the bitch will be mated by a number of males, not always necessarily by the most dominant ones of the group. Finally the bitch becomes less willing to stand and starts to drive away the dogs which, as her sexual odor wanes, gradually disperse.

The dog is a social animal rather than a solitary one. Social living needs signals understood by other members of the group to prevent indiscriminate fighting, disruptive to the

pack as a whole. Facial expression, body posture and tail movement are all clues to the dog's state of mind.

The casual meeting of two male dogs follows a prescribed ritual. After a brief pause to inspect each other at a distance, they will trot toward each other with head up, ears erect and tail held high. Each will circle around sniffing each other's hindquarters, before breaking off the encounter to urinate over the nearest vertical surface, and going on their way.

Ritual inspection

A puppy submits to a
strange adult.

If the meeting takes place between a dog and a bitch, the encounter may be different. Any bitch which is not in season may drive off a strange dog. She may snap, growl and chase it, but rarely does or intends any serious harm. It is abnormal behavior for a dog to attack a bitch, and serious fighting between dogs of different sexes is rare. The bloodiest battles are between bitch and bitch or two male animals.

Puppies, too, are safe from the attack of adults. A very young puppy, when sniffed at by a strange adult dog, will

Nervous posture

roll over onto its back in a gesture of submission. Presenting the vulnerable throat to an opponent in this fashion inhibits the threatened attack.

The nervous dog gives the impression of being smaller than it really is. The ears are laid back and the body is held in a partially crouching attitude. The tail is held tightly between the legs, and such an animal will always keep the head toward the threatened danger and not allow another dog to sniff the anal region. If flight is not possible, the defensive animal will be forced into threatening attitudes. The teeth will be bared and the dog will snap toward its opponent, although unless the attack is pressed home it may not actually bite.

The aggressive, dominant dog presents quite a different picture. Everything combines to make it seem larger than real life. The head is held high and the ears are up. The hair along the spine stands on end and the tail is held rigid in a straight line with the back. The whole body becomes stiff and tense, which increases the impression of size. Such an animal will circle its opponent with a stiff, stilted walk while eyeing it with a fixed glare. This movement contrasts sharply with the high-stepping trot of the more casual encounter. When an aggressive, dominant animal is about to attack, the mouth is slightly opened and the muzzle is wrinkled vertically to show the teeth. The threat is accentuated with growls and snarls, although some breeds will often attack silently.

Aggressive posture

A dog may, of course, attack from a distance. Here the attacker will freeze into a posture with the head held low and level with the back-line. The tip of the rigid tail may wag very slowly from side to side. Some dogs sink down until they are prone before making the attacking charge. This charge usually ends in a body-slamming technique designed to throw the opponent off its feet and expose the vulnerable throat. In a sparring match to establish supremacy in a group of animals, one dog may submit by lying on its side or back, voluntarily exposing its throat. The dominant animal will stand over it threateningly, but is inhibited from actual attack by this gesture of submission.

Dog fights vary in intensity. A half-hearted encounter can often be stopped by dousing the animals with a bucket of water. In a serious fight it is practically impossible to stop it single-handed. Two people grabbing the hind legs of the combatants simultaneously and shaking vigorously may succeed, but only if neither animal has a good grip on its enemy. A dog

This attitude is often followed by attack.

that is hanging on must be choked off, either by twisting the collar tourniquet fashion, or by applying something like smelling salts to the nostrils. Anyone bitten should get immediate medical attention.

One of the effects of domestication is to prolong juvenile behavior, and many adult dogs will play like puppies. An invitation to play is unmistakable and usually irresistible. The forequarters are bowed with the front legs parallel to the ground, while the tail is jauntily curled over the back.

Invitation to play

Bed-making

Many other aspects of dog behavior are related to the lives led by their wild ancestors. In situations of stress many individuals will seek a hole or corner where they feel safer from surprise attack; the dog that disappears under the table at the sound of thunder is an example. Some dogs always choose to sleep in a corner or with their backs to a wall. Therefore, if you are leaving your dog for a short while in the open, either by tying it up or making it stay, it is much kinder to do so

Rolling

in the shelter of a hedge or building, or under a seat, than in the middle of an empty space. No wild animal would lie down and relax in a totally exposed position.

The circling, trampling and scratching movements which many dogs make before they lie down to sleep have two possible explanations. One is that such movements originally served to flatten a small area of concealing vegetation. The other is that the circling movements ended with the dog comfortably positioned with its back to the prevailing wind.

Obviously the patterns of behavior which enable a bitch to care for her puppies are instinctive. Complete lack of interest in the puppies after their birth, or failure to clean and warm them, is abnormal behavior. Some owners do not understand that a bitch who regurgitates half-digested food for her litter when they are about three weeks old or so is also behaving perfectly naturally.

Finally, mention must be made of the habit some dogs have of rolling in anything odoriferous that takes their fancy. No reasonable explanation for this has yet been found. In the opinion of the author it is behavior which seems to occur more often with bitches, but many animals never do it at all. In emergencies, tomato juice on the offending area is a good, temporary deodorant.

Bitch regurgitating for her puppies

TRAINING

The results of recent American research on puppy development has given us a number of clues as to how environment in infancy can affect an adult animal's behavior. In particular, scientists have established the critical periods in a puppy's life for future development.

Up to three weeks of age, environment can only affect a puppy's physical development, not its mental one. From three to seven weeks, the brain and nervous system are developing to adult capacity. During this period a puppy needs the rough and tumble of family life with mother and litter-mates, if its relationship with other dogs when adult is to be a normal one. It is suggested that the best time to form a man/dog relationship is between the seventh and twelfth week. This is best done by removing each puppy in turn from the litter and giving it individual attention. The length of time and the frequency of this personal attention do not matter as much as the regularity, which is important. The result of leaving a puppy kenneled with other dogs but without individual

Young puppies need human contact.

human care until the age of 6 weeks, will be a permanent limitation on the animal's ability to respond to training.

The value of recognizing what is instinctive in a dog's behavior helps one to realize both the limitations and the possibilities of training. Man has always selected and adapted and strengthened a dog's instinctive behavior for the specialized work he wants the dog to do. The retriever carrying the dead bird back to its master is paralleled in nature by the wolf carrying food home for her cubs. The tense stance of a pointer revealing the presence of game and the hypnotic glare of the Border Collie controlling sheep are both refinements on the hunting techniques of the dog's wild ancestors.

Retriever with pheasant (above).
Border Collie showing 'eye' (below)

Training should begin
at an early age.

Domestic training

A very few people are 'natural' animal trainers who can teach an animal practically anything, apparently with little effort. A very few people cannot establish any relationship with their dog and teach it anything at all. The majority of dog owners fall between the two extremes and muddle along with a good deal of wasted effort. Training consists of building up a series of conditioned reflexes, or repeating a command followed by an appropriate action until a habit is formed. This needs patience and self-control on the owner's part, and some attention and concentration from the dog. This is the reason why the more advanced and complicated training, such as is given to policy and guide dogs, is not started until the animal is a year or eighteen months old.

In another sense, of course, puppies are learning from their surroundings all the time, and here a little thought on the part of the owner can lay the foundations for a well-mannered, adult dog. The most important thing is to prevent the formation of bad habits. If you do not want your dog to chase the cat, bark at the postman or sleep on the beds, discourage him from the outset. The amusement of watching a tiny puppy trying to climb into an armchair is apt to turn to unreasonable anger when the same animal, six months older and covered in mud, flings itself on the cushions.

There are two things which one can start to teach a puppy as soon as one owns it. The first is its own name, which it should always associate with pleasure. Always reward it lavishly for coming to its name, either by feeding it or by plentiful praise. The feeding of tidbits as a reward is not something to be continued throughout the dog's life. A dog that only comes when it sees food is not an asset, but tidbits are an invaluable aid when teaching a young and greedy puppy its name. The second basic word to teach a pup is the word 'No'. This, in effect, means 'Stop what you are doing', so when you start using the word 'No' make sure you can and do enforce it. The puppy who is chewing the rug will ignore the command to leave it alone unless you are prepared to get up and see that it does—and as soon as it does, whether because you made it or because it began to understand, enthusiastic praise from you will help drive the lesson home.

Buying a collar and lead is probably one of the first things any owner does. For a puppy, where both are likely to be outgrown, cheap and lightweight articles are perfectly satisfactory. Many people like a collar on their dog at all times, but some of the more ornamental collars will not stand up to a sudden sharp strain. A bolt and spring clip is best on the end of a lead. Those where the opening comes at the point of most strain should be avoided. Leather or nylon leads are good. Although chains are strong, some owners find them uncomfortable. The neck-frill of a long-haired dog will be permanently marked if it wears a collar constantly.

Serious training is always done on a slip collar, and many people prefer them as they give more control. A slip collar consists of a chain with a ring at either end. The chain is dropped through one of the rings to form a loop which is put over the dog's head. A jerk on the collar is uncomfortable for the dog, but when the lead is slack the collar is loose. This will only happen if the collar is put on correctly. The dog should walk on the left hand side of the owner, and the ring through which the chain is slipping should be underneath.

Many dogs express their pleasure and excitement by jumping up. The earlier this habit is checked the easier it is to cure. A slight push with your foot will unbalance a puppy which should be praised only when its four feet are on the ground. With an adult a knee brought up as the dog is jumping will discourage it from the attempt. As with most training the timing is everything.

A raised knee will discourage a dog from jumping up.

Nothing is more liable to sour good neighborly relations than having a dog that barks and howls everytime you are out. Again it is much easier to teach a puppy to remain quiet when alone, than to attempt to train a dog that has already got into the habit of barking. Shut the puppy up for a short while every day and scold any whimpers of discontent through the door. Do not go back in or the dog may get the idea that it has only got to make a noise for you to reappear. Silence should be rewarded by release and praise.

Many pet owners are worried by having a dog which will not come when called. There is no easy answer to this problem, which arises with all dogs at some time or other. A dog's ability to associate ideas is very limited, so you must be very sure that the dog always associates coming in answer to its name with something pleasant. If you call a dog to you and then punish it for some previous misdemeanor, it will associate the punishment with coming to you and be more wary next time. If you only call your dog to you at the end of a free run in order to put it on the lead, it will associate coming to you with the end of freedom and will tend to avoid you instead. In the first example, it is much better to praise the dog for coming and then lead it to the scene of its crime

Crouching will often encourage a dog to come.

50

and scold it there. In the second, if you call it a number of times during the walk, praise it for coming and then let it go again, it will be less likely to connect coming to you with the end of its freedom. Never attempt to grab or chase a dog. Training is often a battle of wits and will-power. Never let it become a battle of speed and agility or the dog will win every time.

One of the most useful things a pet can learn is to stay and wait for its owner. This is one of the exercises taught for obedience competition work and the method of teaching it is discussed on later pages.

Well-trained dogs can be taken shopping.

Most animals enjoy accompanying their owners in the car, and it is worthwhile training the dog so that the other passengers also enjoy the ride. Make the dog stay beside the car, even if the door is open, until you tell it to get in. Decide where the dog should sit, whether on one particular seat or the floor, and make it stay there. Most dogs take the opening of a car door to mean that they can catapult themselves out onto the road. A well-trained dog will wait until it is told to get out. Many dogs like to put their heads out of the window when the car is moving, but this can lead to serious eye and ear trouble. Barking at passers-by or other dogs can be a disagreeable habit which should be discouraged early. If you have to leave your dog in the car make sure it is parked in the shade with adequate ventilation. Small metal grilles can be bought that can be fitted over an open window to allow enough fresh air.

Car-sickness is a problem usually caused by apprehension. If you have a dog that gets car-sick try not to feed it for several hours before a journey. Puppies very often grow out of this condition. Sometimes short daily journeys terminating in a good gallop in the fresh air before the dog really has time to be ill, will effect a cure. Sedatives and travel-sickness pills may be prescribed by your vet. Keep newspaper in the car in case of an emergency.

Many people buy a dog as a guard as well as a companion. The guarding instinct is undeveloped in puppies, and any youngster who is suspicious of strangers is either nervous or will be too aggressive when adult. A dog's protective instincts appear with maturity, and it is impossible to generalize as to when this will happen. In some cases it never happens at all, but even if you have the type which loves everyone, it can still be made useful. Always take the dog with you when you open the door to a caller. Make it lie down and stay in the hall where it can watch the proceedings. If there is a stranger on the doorstep, the very presence of an immobile dog will act as a deterrent to anyone with evil intentions. If you are greeting friends, allow the dog to greet them too. Teach it to discriminate between sounds as well. The dog that reacts to a muffled footstep is of value as a guard: the one that barks when the bell rings is not.

A dog's protective instincts appear with maturity.

This sort of specialized training should only be undertaken by experts.

Specialized training

A well-trained dog can be taken practically anywhere without being a nuisance to itself or others. Most dogs enjoy learning, provided the lessons are kept short and the trainer is enthusiastic with praise for their achievements. A couple of ten-minute training periods a day are better than a solid half hour when the dog's attention is liable to wander. Try to ensure that all lessons end happily, and on the days when the dog seems unnecessarily stupid and you feel irritable,

One exercise in an Obedience Competition

cut the whole thing short and try again later. A good trainer has something in common with an actor, for dogs are very sensitive to a tone of voice. All commands should be given in a firm, no-nonsense tone. If the dog does not obey it is unlikely to be because it has not heard, so all shouting should be reserved for emergencies. Your aim should be to get the dog to obey you the first time, so if you have to repeat the command, make sure you enforce it at the same time. Praise should be immediate and enthusiastic, whether the dog has done what you wanted by accident, or because you man-handled it or because it understood you. Correction should also be immediate, with a disapproving growl in the voice. Avoid a high-pitched nagging tone as it is a lot less effective.

All dogs are individuals, and methods of training which work with one may fail with another. Training routines should be flexible and varied because an interested and attentive dog is much easier to teach. Training classes are held in many places, and these are invaluable in teaching a dog to obey you whatever the distractions are around it. They also provide expert advice. Your problem, which may seem unique and insoluble, is unlikely to be either, and much help can be gained from such classes.

Obedience Competitions are held in a number of countries. These are tests graded in difficulty, where each dog performs a number of set exercises and is marked on the style and standard of the work. In the United States only purebred dogs may take part, but in Britain any animal may compete, provided its name has been recorded on the Obedience Register at the Kennel Club.

Heeling is the basic exercise which is included in every competition. The aim is to have the dog walking at your left side with its head close to and even with your left leg. However you twist or turn, or whatever your pace, the dog should maintain its position, and whenever you halt it should sit smartly beside you.

When you are teaching something new, choose a quiet spot where you have freedom to move in any direction and the dog has no distractions. The dog should be on a lead and a slip collar. Take the lead in your right hand, have the dog on your left side and tell it to 'Sit'. As you do so, keep its head up with the lead and press its haunches down with your left hand. When it is in the right position, praise it but do not let it move. Then give the command 'Heel' and walk straight ahead, giving a slight jerk on the lead to encourage the dog to follow. Always try to keep the lead loose by encouraging the dog to stay close with your left hand. When it gets out of position, jerk it back with the lead and praise it as soon as it is in the right place. Make it sit

'Stay'

'Heel'

every time you stop. Try heeling off the lead only when the dog will stay beside you without the need for correction.

To be able to leave a dog in one place to wait until you return has many practical advantages. As you have already taught it to sit, start teaching it to stay in a sitting position until you tell it to get up. Get the dog sitting beside you. While giving the command 'Stay' take one step in front of it so that you are facing it with hand upraised. If it moves put it back and repeat until it understands. The 'Down-stay' and the 'Stand-stay' can be taught in the same manner, but each must be perfect before going on to the next.

In the 'Recall' the dog comes and sits in front of the owner.

When you have taught the dog to remain sitting, you can go on to the recall. Again this is taught on the lead, and this is why a six-foot-long lead is recommended for training purposes. Leave the dog sitting, go to the end of the lead and turn to face it. Call the dog to you, encouraging it with your voice and the lead, and make it sit squarely in front of you. At the command 'Heel', it should go behind you and sit at your left side.

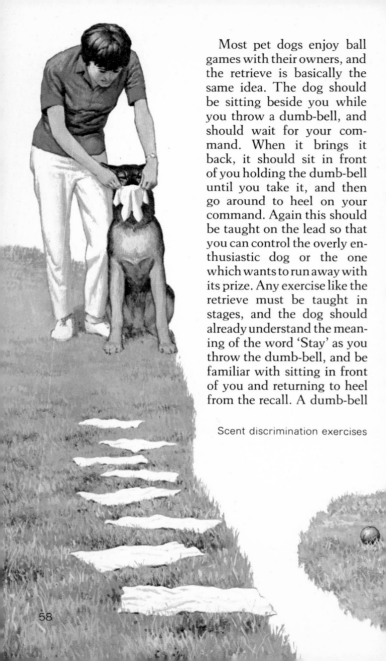

Most pet dogs enjoy ball games with their owners, and the retrieve is basically the same idea. The dog should be sitting beside you while you throw a dumb-bell, and should wait for your command. When it brings it back, it should sit in front of you holding the dumb-bell until you take it, and then go around to heel on your command. Again this should be taught on the lead so that you can control the overly enthusiastic dog or the one which wants to run away with its prize. Any exercise like the retrieve must be taught in stages, and the dog should already understand the meaning of the word 'Stay' as you throw the dumb-bell, and be familiar with sitting in front of you and returning to heel from the recall. A dumb-bell

Scent discrimination exercises

is a standard piece of obedience equipment, and it is important either to buy or make one the right size and weight for your dog. If you have a dog that enjoys having things thrown for it, teaching the retrieve will be much easier. If your animal merely looks blankly at you when you throw something, you will have to start with the more basic step of teaching it to hold something in its mouth when you tell it to. Many dogs are reluctant to take anything into their mouth at first, so it is important to place it there with as little force as necessary and to give plenty of praise. When the dog will take an article from your hand and hold it, teach it to pick it up and gradually progress to throwing it. Once it is reliable with the dumb-bell, vary the articles.

Scent discrimination is where the dog is required to search through a miscellany of articles and bring back the one with your scent on it. A more advanced exercise is where the dog is given a stranger's scent and has to pick out an article with a matching odor. In American competition work, the handlers are required to provide all the articles used in this exercise. In Britain, the judge provides the articles. In each case the handler is given one article to rub between his hands in order to scent it, and this article is then taken by the ring steward, who is careful not to touch it, and placed among a random miscellany of objects at the other side of the ring. The handler cups his hand around the dog's nose to remind it of the scent and sends it to retrieve the object.

The 'Send away' is an exercise scheduled in British Obedience Competitions and Working Trials in order to demonstrate a handler's control over a dog's movements in the distance. In the obedience exercise the handler has to send the dog to a particular spot very often marked by a box on the ground. The dog has to lie down and stay there until recalled to heel, so if your dog is only used to lying down beside you, the first requirement is that it should be taught to drop on command wherever it may be in relation to you. The American Open Obedience Test requires a drop on recall, where the handler, at a signal from the judge, orders the dog to drop as it is returning. The more advanced Working Trials specify that not only should the handler be able to send the dog in a straight line away from him, but he should also be able to direct a dog to go right or left at a distance. This exercise is derived from the practical experience of working gundogs and police dogs.

Distant control exercise, another English Obedience Competition, has little practical application. The handler,

The 'Send away'

who must be at least ten paces from the dog, orders the animal to 'Sit', 'Stand' and lie 'Down'. Any movement of the dog from the given spot is penalized. As many dogs tend to shuffle forward during the sequence of movements, some owners position the dog on a low box, which effectively prevents forward movement, during training. Some dogs tend to muddle the sit and the stand because they move on hearing the first sibilant. The remedy is to replace one of the two commands by a hand signal.

Though the more advanced exercises seem impossibly difficult to a novice trainer, the more you teach a dog success-

Distance control exercise

fully the easier it becomes. You must maintain a dog's confidence and enthusiasm, and this is more easily done if training sessions are kept short enough for neither of you to become bored. Always understand clearly what you want the dog to do and how you are going to achieve this before you start training. Teach only one thing at a time, and remember that many training problems can be solved by going back to the basics with the dog on the lead.

Obedience Competitions have become more and more popular, but have also come in for a fair amount of criticism. Some people concentrate solely on teaching their dogs the set exercises, and their dogs, away from the show, are allowed to behave as badly as any completely untrained animal. Anything a dog is taught should be put to use in day-to-day living as much as possible. Critics also insist that rigorous obedience training turns dogs into automata, unable to react to anything except the next command. This unfortunate impression is reinforced by the sight of handlers maintaining an unnaturally wooden exterior, lest an involuntary movement should be interpreted and penalized as an extra command to the dog.

Working Trials are held in Britain under Kennel Club rules. These too are graded for difficulty, and instead of the outright win needed in Obedience Competitions, any dog that gets more than 70 percent of the marks in each section, can qualify with the appropriate letters after its name. Those

Agility tests

62

gaining 80 percent or over can add 'excellent' to the title.

The Companion Dog (C.D.) Stake consists of heeling, exercises to establish control, tests for agility, retrieving and scent work.

In the Utility Dog (U.D.) Stake, Working Dog (W.D.) Stake, Tracking Dog (T.D.) Stake and Police Dog (P.D.) Stake, both searching an area to find hidden articles and tracking are included, as well as exercises to demonstrate the handler's control of the dog, and agility tests. The dogs must show steadiness to gunshot, and bark and cease barking on command. The P.D. Stake has a section on manwork, training for which is best left to professionals, but which is spectacular to watch. P.D. dogs are required to quarter the ground to find a hidden person, refuse food from a stranger and defend their handlers from attack. They must pursue and detain a 'criminal' and, perhaps most important of all, leave the pursuit or attack when commanded to do so.

Though the more advanced Working Trials need considerable training experience, the C.D. Stake should be within the capabilities of most dogs and their owners. Unfortunately some breeds will be automatically excluded by the nature of

Food refusal

the agility tests, which consist of jumps, the height of which is geared solely to the height of the dog at the shoulder. Any dog over fifteen inches at the shoulder is required to scale jump six feet, which rules out the extra-large, heavy breeds. There are actually three jumps required of a C.D. dog. For an animal exceeding fifteen inches at the shoulder, there is a scale jump of six feet (i.e., a solid board wall which a dog will get over by a combination of springing and scrambling). The clear jump will be three feet in height and the long jump will have a spread of nine feet. It is obvious from these figures that the first requirement of success is to have a really fit dog. It is impossible to *make* a dog jump an obstacle of any size, so it is essential it should enjoy the process from the start. As with teaching any other exercise the early stages should be on the lead, with jumps so low that they represent no obstacle at all to the dog. Your pleasure and praise for its performance will encourage it to make the greater efforts required as the lead is taken off and the jumps progressively raised.

65

The Americans include jumping in their Open and Utility Obedience tests. They are scaled so that no breed is really excluded. The dogs are asked to jump only one and a half times their own height, or three feet, whichever is less. The massive breeds, such as Newfoundlands or St. Bernards have only to jump a hurdle their own height. Dogs are, however, expected to retrieve a dumb-bell over a hurdle and complete a long jump of up to six feet. In the Utility Class the dog is required to go out between two jumps and come back in to the handler over either jump at his command.

Possibly the most useful obedience exercise in the American schedule is what is called the 'Stand for examination'. The idea behind this is that the dog must stay still on your command and allow itself to be examined by a stranger, without showing resentment or fear. Not only is this excellent training for a dog which may be going into the show ring, but it is also a useful control to have when you are grooming your

The 'Stand for examination' is one of the American obedience exercises.

dog, or taking it for a health check by your veterinary surgeon. If this exercise is slowly and sympathetically taught, nervous dogs often gain more confidence by it, and aggressive dogs gain more control. The dog should be first taught the 'Stand-stay' and remain still while you leave it in any direction, going away for ten yards or so and staying away for up to a minute. Your dog should get used to your returning, giving it a hand to sniff and then touching it lightly all over. Gradually make your examination more thorough, including looking at its teeth, running your hands down its legs, and pressing lightly on its hindquarters to test its steadiness. Someone else, well known to the dog, should then give the same sort of examination, while you stand near, holding the dog on the end of a loose lead and reassuring it, should it be at all apprehensive. Then get a complete stranger to the dog to follow the same procedure. If you are worried about your dog's reaction at this stage, stand up close to it, ready to correct with the lead or encourage with the voice. Teaching a

Retrieving a dumb-bell over a jump is another American Obedience Test exercise.

GROUND SCENT

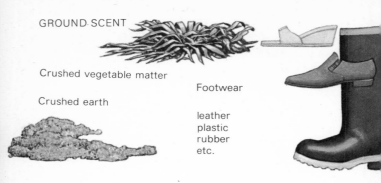

Crushed vegetable matter

Crushed earth

Footwear

leather
plastic
rubber
etc.

dog to track or to search for and find missing articles and persons is something that can give a greater thrill of achievement than almost anything else. Most dogs are capable of tracking, and what distinguishes a good tracker from an indifferent one is more the quality of enthusiasm for the job than any difference in physical make-up. It is vital, therefore, when starting to teach your dog any sort of nosework, that its early efforts should always be rewarded with success. Make sure you know where the missing article is hidden or exactly where the track went, so that, if necessary, you can urge your dog step by step in the right direction until it accomplishes the task. Early success leads to the dog making greater and greater efforts.

We know a little of what constitutes a scent that a dog can follow. The ground scent will include the smell of disturbed earth and bruised vegetation, as well as footwear.

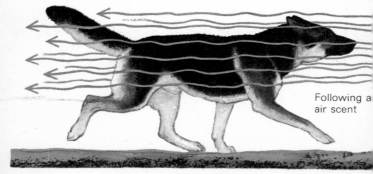

Following a
air scent

AIR SCENT
Human

sex
occupation
sweat
etc.

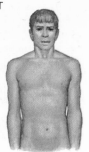

Clothing

wool
cotton
plastic
leather
etc.

Obviously the terrain has a great deal to do with the durability and strength of the track. A track across ploughed earth or through long grass will be easier to follow. Tracking across rock or concrete is practically impossible. The passage of a body through the air also leaves a wind-borne scent. This will consist of the individual odor of sex, clothing and so on. This wind-borne scent can be followed by a dog with its nose up, and a steady breeze may move it from its original position, so that a dog may follow someone by following a wind-borne scent several feet to one side of the original track. This can also lead to a dog cutting corners rather than following the original track around a bend. In both these deviations there is the danger that the dog will miss finding any article left by the tracklayer. Scent evaporates, so the durability of a track is greatly affected by the weather. In general, mild weather and sheltered ground are best.

Following a
ground scent

Though it is not necessary for a tracking dog to have been taught the entire course of obedience exercises, you must start with a dog that retrieves with enthusiasm. The 'Seek back', where the dog learns to find something that you have dropped while walking along, is of obvious practical importance.

Use an article that the dog is familiar with and has retrieved before. As the dog is walking beside you, drop the article, continue a few steps and turn around and send the dog to fetch it. At this stage the article should be clearly visible, and it does not matter if the dog works by sight. Increase the distance very gradually and always in a straight line until you are sure the dog has understood that what it is

looking for is somewhere along the line you have traveled. Once it back-tracks reliably in a straight line, you can make your course more complicated.

Before teaching a dog to search an area of ground for hidden articles, you need an animal which will retrieve and which you can control at a distance. It is important, too, that you use a distinctly separate command for each type of scent exercise. In Britain, in the C.D. Stake at a Working Trial, the dog will be required to search an area of ground roughly 12 yards square, and it will have a time limit of two minutes to find an article with the owner's scent on it. As the owner is not allowed to enter the search area himself, he must be able to direct the dog's movement from a distance.

Laying a drag

A tracking dog wears a harness usually made of webbing, to which is attached a leash at least 30 feet long. In practice, this is to allow a dog to maneuver and cast around for a track, without the handler having to get in the way and muddy the scent still further. In case the unfamiliarity of the harness bothers the dog, get it used to wearing it beforehand. After this, keep the harness for tracking sessions only, so that it associates one with the other. Choose, if possible, a flat, open space with short grass and no obstacles, and do not let your dog romp all over it beforehand. Equip yourself with

Start of a hound trail

a familiar object which the dog will retrieve with pleasure.

The direction of the wind should be studied so that the dog will be working into the wind after the track is laid. The dog should be left in the down position, where it can see your actions, and it should be shown the object you wish it to find. The start of the track should be made by treading heavily in one spot to provide a good scenting place. Then walk heavily in a straight line for about five yards, place the object on the ground, making sure that the dog can see what you are doing, and return along the same path to the animal. Lead the dog quickly to the start of the track and encourage it to sniff the ground there with the command 'Seek'. The dog should be eager to bring back the object you left and should receive enthusiastic praise for doing so. The fact that it does not have to use its nose in the early stages of this training is immaterial. As soon as it realizes that you want it to bring back the dropped article, the tracks can be gradually lengthened until it will be forced to put its nose down to find what you want. From this elementary beginning, further training will include the gradual introduction of bends in the track, more than one article to be found, a delay between the track being laid and the dog being asked to follow it, cross-tracks being placed (which the dog should ignore), and as many different types of terrain as possible.

SHOWING DOGS

Very many people obtain a great deal of pleasure from the hobby of showing dogs. The first dog show was held in Britain, at Newcastle, in 1859. Pointers and setters were the only breeds entered, but the idea was a success from the start and an increasing number of shows followed fairly rapidly.

With the popularity of showing, a divergence began to appear between the dogs which worked and which were bred for their ability to do so, and the dogs which were shown and bred solely for looks. The show ring has constantly been criticized for producing beauties without brains, and it is true that in some breeds the physical peculiarities have been exaggerated to such an extent that the dogs appear caricatures of their working forebears. However, in an increasingly urbanized society, fewer and fewer dogs are required to work, and many breeds have been standardized and improved greatly in appearance by being shown. Also, a number of breeds whose original job no longer exists would have become extinct but for the interest of show exhibitors.

The American Kennel Club, founded in 1878, recognizes 117 pure breeds of dogs whose pedigrees it records and certifies. Such dogs are known as 'pure-bred' or 'registered.' For each breed there is an official Standard of Perfection.

In each ring, a judge, whose qualifications and assignments have been approved by the AKC, will compare the entries with a mental image of this Standard — standing and moving — and with each other. Each breed has its own type and balance which distinguishes it from other breeds. The skeletal structure of each dog is examined, as well as its muscular development and its coordination as shown by its gait from the front, side and rear. Consideration is also given to coat, color, condition, expression, temperament and a quality of elegance or style.

To simplify judging, entries in each sex are divided into five regular classes — Puppy, Novice, Bred-by-Exhibit, American-bred and Open. In each class the judge will place the winners in front of boards marked 1, 2, 3 and 4, and he will award blue, red, yellow and white ribbons accordingly, along with whatever prize money and trophies have been offered for these placings. In breeds of small entries, all classes may not be represented.

Blue-ribbon winners are then compared for a 'winners dog', which receives a purple ribbon and 'points' toward championship according to the schedule printed in the catalog. To earn the title 'Champion', a dog must win a minimum of 15 points of which two must be 'major' awards of three to five points under different judges. A third judge must award at

Breeds change: Scottish Terriers of 1910 and the 1960's

least one of the remaining points. A move-up reserve is also selected for a purple-and-white ribbon. After the male (dog) classes have been judged, there are corresponding classes for females (bitches) leading to 'winners bitch' and reserve. The 'winners dog' and 'winners bitch' then compete with champions from previous shows in a Best-of-Breed competition for a purple-and-gold rosette and trophy. If neither Winners Dog nor Winners Bitch is chosen for Best of Breed they then compete for Best of Winners and a blue-and-white ribbon. An award is also made for the best entry of the opposite sex, which receives a red-and-white rosette. Some breeds are divided into 'Varieties' by color (Cocker Spaniels, Bull Terriers, English Toy Spaniels); size (Beagles, Manchesters, Poodles); or by coats (Fox Terriers, Dachshunds, Collies, Chihuahuas). Each of these is judged as if a separate breed.

Group Judging
Top winners of these breeds and varieties are then eligible to compete in groups: I-Sporting; II-Hounds; III-Working; IV-Terrier; V-Toy; and VI-Non-Sporting. The judges determine how closely each breed winner approaches its breed's standard of perfection and how it performs as a show dog. Blue rosettes and trophies are awarded group winners, followed by red, yellow and white rosettes. Finally the winners of the six groups compete for the top award of Best of All Breeds in Show, designated by a red-white-and-blue rosette and trophy.

Junior Showmanship

There are Junior Showmanship classes in which boys and girls from 10 to 16 years of age demonstrate their skills at handling dogs in conformation competition for ribbons and trophies.

Obedience Competition

Obedience competition starts with Novice Class exercises—heeling on leash, standing for examination, heel free, recall, long sit, long down, leading to the Competition Dog degree, C.D.; Open Class competition adds drop on recall, retrieve on flat, over jump, broad jump, for Companion Dog Excellent, C.D.X. The most difficult Utility Class adds the following exercises: scent discrimination, seek back, signal exercise, directed jumping and group examination, for Utility Dog, U.D. A separate exercise in tracking, held apart from the dog show, leads to an additional letter 'T' for Tracking. All three classes of obedience competition demonstrate the dog's mastery of training, making it a better canine citizen in the home and in public.

In judging obedience, dogs are scored on accuracy and smartness of performance of each exercise. Ribbons, prizes and trophies are awarded for highest total scores. An obedience degree requires three credits of at least 170 of a perfect 200 score and not less than 50 percent of any exercise.

Open class

Most dog magazines advertise forthcoming shows, and owners wishing to enter should write to the show secretary for a premium list, which lists the classes available, judges, and so on, and an entry form. The owner fills this in and returns it with the entry fee before the closing date for entries for that show. The definition of the classes available for your particular breed will be printed in the premium list, so that you can decide which one your dog is eligible for. Because of the distances involved, many American dogs are shown by professional handlers, while in Britain most owners show their own exhibits.

(*Above*) Benching at a show. Pekinese are traditionally shown on a table in Britain.

As a dog show is a beauty competition, your aim should be to present a sparklingly clean, well-groomed animal with the bloom and vigor of perfect health, and the confidence and discipline to show itself to the best advantage. If you are a novice exhibitor, a visit to one or two shows beforehand will familiarize you with the procedure and the particular techniques which may be used to show your breed. If you are taking a puppy to its first show, choose one of the smaller, more informal events and do your best to see that it enjoys the experience. A number of dogs never show well throughout their life because of a frightening experience at their first dog show.

Exercising like this should only be done in moderation.

Some breeds should be
bathed shortly before
show competition.

To show successfully you must first have a dog in perfect
health. The basics here are a good nutritious diet, freedom from
external and internal parasites, and adequate exercise to give a
good muscle tone. For your own peace of mind the dog should
also be fully inoculated, with up-to-date booster shots if necessary, before being taken to any show. If you have a breed where
length and abundance of coat are important you will cer-
tainly have to restrict the dog's galloping over rough country
or through undergrowth, as this will pull out too much
coat. One of the best forms of exercise is walking the dog
on a hard surface. Not only will this accustom it to walking on a loose lead, but it will also improve its feet and hind
movement. A show dog customarily carries a little more
flesh than a working animal, but should never be allowed to
become plump.

Teeth will be examined in the show ring and so any deposits of tartar should be scraped off, either with a dental scaler or the milled edge of a coin. Regular cleaning with a proprietary tooth powder will help to whiten the teeth and preserve them. Nails must be short, and if road-walking has not shortened them sufficiently, they should be clipped or filed, taking care to avoid the quick. Eyes also need attention. If your dog has eyes with a tendency to water, daily bathing with a saline solution (one teaspoonful of salt to a pint of water) will help to prevent unsightly tearstains marking the coat on the day of the event.

Training should be started early. If you are going to a benched show (i.e., one providing a wooden stall where each exhibit must stay except when being judged or exercised), you must have an animal that remains quiet when tied up. A bench chain and leather collar are one of the essentials that you will need for your show bag.

Get your dog used to having its mouth examined.

As well as your dog's conformation, its movement will also be assessed. This is normally done by all the exhibits circling the ring, while the judge remains in the center. Here it is vital to have a dog which will trot beside you on a loose lead, despite the proximity of other dogs. Train your dog to keep its head up, so that it does not pause to sniff around. Remember the judge wants to see the dog so do not get in the way. After examining your animal, the judge will usually ask you to move it in a straight line, so that his front and then hind action can be seen. If you get a friend to walk the dog up and down some time before you show it, you can assess at which speed it moves best, and make a practice of showing it at that speed in the ring. Movement can only be judged on a level, non-slippery surface. It is obvious that a toy dog cannot show its paces on rough, high grass, nor can movement be judged when a dog is going downhill because

Show techniques differ from breed to breed. Here handler readies Welsh Terrier for the judge.

the hindquarters are not being used for propulsion at all when on a down slope.

The judge will want to see and handle the dog while the animal is standing still. Teaching your dog to allow this is done on the lines of teaching the 'Stand for examination' obedience exercise. Teeth will also be examined so this is something else to which your dog should be accustomed. Most judges will request the exhibitor to part the dog's lips so that teeth can be seen. Small dogs are often examined on a table.

Before discussing different grooming techniques needed for various types of coat, it should be emphasized that all dogs benefit from daily coat care. With smooth-coated breeds, a short-bristled brush should be used first, followed by a hound glove or chamois leather to polish the coat. The coat should always be brushed the way it lies and a marvelous sheen can be achieved by stroking repeatedly with the bare hand.

Smooth-coated breeds can be groomed with a hound glove.

Dogs with very heavy wrinkles, such as Bloodhounds, Basset Hounds and Pekinese, should have these crevices kept spotlessly clean and dry as there is a tendency for skin infections to occur there.

Wire-haired breeds need a variety of trimming techniques in which it takes a lot of practice to become expert. The right equipment simplifies the task, and a basic necessity is a grooming table. If you intend to do a number of dogs of differing sizes this should preferably be adjustable in height, as well as being of fairly solid construction. Grooming stands are available which help restrain badly behaved or boisterous dogs. If you can see the dog in a large mirror while you are working, this lets you check the effect you are achieving as you go along. A good photo of a well-trimmed specimen of your particular breed is an invaluable guide line.

Scottish Deerhound

If at all possible wire-haired breeds should not be bathed as this softens the coat, which may take several weeks to get back the required texture. A number of cleansing powders are on the market which are rubbed into the coat and then brushed out, and these are preferable to shampooing. A few harsh-coated breeds need no trimming. These include Deerhounds and Wolfhounds, which should be groomed vigorously with a stiff, medium-bristled brush. In any untrimmed breed like these it may be necessary to remove a few hairs in order to neaten the dog's outline, and this can be done with a pair of blunt-nosed scissors.

Some terriers that only need light trimming include the Cairn, Australian, Border and Norwich. Here again it is the general outline of the dog that needs revealing cleanly by plucking out straggling hairs that spoil the topline. The feet and ears may be neatly trimmed around with scissors.

Bedlington Terriers and Kerry Blue Terriers are in a class of their own, as they are both trimmed entirely with scissors. There, however, the resemblance ends. The Bedlington has a linty coat which is trimmed to look like plush. This is one of the more difficult breeds, as it requires a good eye to sculpture the dog to the right shape. Kerries have a soft, wavy single coat, and care must be taken to get an even finish with no scissor marks showing.

The terrier breeds that require heavy trimming include the Airedale, Lakeland, Welsh, Irish, Scottish, Sealyham and Wire-Haired Fox Terrier. Basically, the coats of terrier breeds like these consist of a harsh, wiry, outer coat, which should be free from curl, and a soft, shorter undercoat. Trimming was originally to remove the old, dead coat and to prevent the dog looking ragged and unkempt during the period that the old coat was shed and the new one was growing. A wild animal will probably shed its coat in the spring and autumn, but this natural rhythm is not so apparent in the domestic dog, which so often lives under conditions including artificial heat and light. Pet terriers very often need their coats stripped out three times a year.

There are two methods of stripping. The pet taken to the dog's beauty parlor will usually have the old coat removed by electric clippers. This is by far the quickest method, and few owners are prepared to pay for the labor involved in hand stripping. The result will look much neater and be at its best two to three weeks afterward, when any marks left by the clippers will have had time to grow out. The old coat will not, of course, have been removed completely by the clippers, merely shortened to expose the undercoat and the new, harsh hair growing through.

The exhibition terrier receives quite different treatment, and professional handlers put in a very great deal of time keeping their terriers in show trim. These experts do most of their trimming by hand, tweaking out a few hairs at a time between finger and thumb. Powdered chalk in the coat helps them to get a grip, but plucking the hair by this method is quite easy, though tedious, when the coat is ready to fall. With terriers that are exhibited regularly, trimming is a continuous business, with the dog's coat kept in as near perfect condition as possible with daily attention. The coat of an untrimmed dog destined for a show career should be taken in hand at least three months before the dog is expected to make its debut. Large areas, such as the topline and flanks may be dealt with by using a stripping knife. At least one lesson in trimming your own breed from a professional is recommended.

Airedale

Breeds with silky coats can be shampooed more frequently without harming the texture of the hair. Such breeds include the Afghan, Borzoi, setters and spaniels, all of which benefit by bathing before a show, provided the right shampoo (i.e., one that leaves a natural sheen) is used. The bath should be a tepid one, and household detergent or strong soaps should not be used as washing agents. Before bathing, the dog's ears should be plugged with cotton, and a smear of vaseline around the eyes will help to keep the soap out. The depth of the water should be roughly half-way up the dog's legs, and the animal should be wetted all over except for the head. This is easier with a spray, though a sponge or large pot will do the job. Only after the body has been lathered should the head be done, and if a spray is not available to remove the

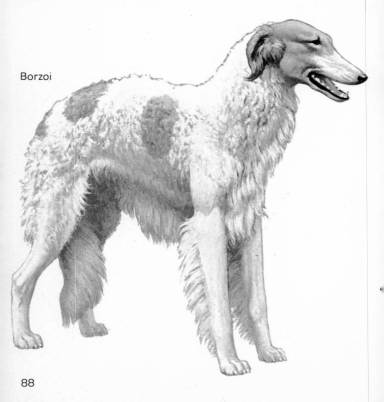

Borzoi

soap, then two or three changes of rinsing water will be necessary. As much water should be squeezed out of the coat as possible and then a towel should be pinned loosely around the dog's body before it is allowed to shake. A smooth-haired dog can be toweled almost completely dry, but a hair dryer or fan heater of some sort is an invaluable aid for any breed with a more profuse coat. If you have a breed where the hair must be straight, brushing flat during the final stages of drying will help prevent any wave from developing.

The type of trimming acceptable in the show ring for setters and the various spaniels differs from country to country. Profuse feathering on the legs however is required, and can be encouraged by daily wetting with cold water, followed by brisk massage and a light dressing of olive oil.

English Setter

Where profuseness of coat is a desired breed feature, care must be taken not to break or drag out the hair by using the wrong grooming tools. Old English Sheepdogs should have any mats removed gently with the coarsest comb obtainable. Brushing is beneficial, but the brush should be chosen with bristles long enough to penetrate but not harsh enough to break the hair. All breeds with very heavy coats should be trained to lie on their sides while the hair is brushed in layers an inch or so at a time. As with all grooming, if this is done gently and regularly, the dog will enjoy rather than resent it.

Breeds with stand-off coats such as Collies, Shetland

Sheepdogs, Samoyeds and Chows, may look soft and fluffy from a distance but actually have an outer coat of coarse, harsh hair which feels crisp to the touch. This type of coat should be brushed with the grain as well as against it, and the final grooming should aim at making the coat stand up as much as possible. The outer coat is supported by a thick, dense, wooly undercoat, and care must be taken not to comb too much of this out.

Many dog breeders have their own theories as to how to produce a long and profuse coat. Most of these remain unproven, and it would seem that the best way to get a heavily coated animal is to breed for coat in exactly the same way as breeding for other physical features. Obviously, poor nourishment or ill-health will affect a coat adversely, and there is some evidence to suggest that a proportion of fat in the diet may be beneficial for the skin and hair. Dogs kept in outdoor kennels without artificial light follow a more natural pattern of shedding and growth, and this steady growth period may have advantages over the haphazard molt induced by artificial lighting.

The popularity of the Poodle means that it is a breed that more than any other is liable to suffer from coat neglect. Even if you pay to have your Poodle clipped at regular intervals, daily grooming is still a must. The best brush for a coat which should have a good hard texture, is a whalebone

Pomeranian

one, and the comb should be one with medium teeth. Poodles are not prone to shed their hair onto the surroundings, but the old coat must be combed out or else it forms impenetrable mats. As with all long-coat breeds, these are most likely to form just behind the ears, inside the elbows, under the stomach and inside the thighs. Any mats should be teased out gently with comb and fingers. Only cut them as a last resort as it will take months for the resulting scar to grow out of the coat. No heavy-coated breed should ever be bathed until it has been thoroughly groomed first, as small tangles quickly felt into larger ones when the dog is lathered. Any long tags of hair spoiling the outline of the dog can be snipped off using scissors and comb.

There are a number of styles for clipping a Poodle, and anyone wishing to experiment can buy books devoted to the subject. A basic requirement is a good pair of electric clippers which must be kept clean, sharp and well oiled. At least three different blades will be required, remembering that the

higher the blade number the closer the clip. Poodles are generally introduced to the clippers between two to three months of age. It is a good idea to stroke the puppy with the clippers switched off at first. This can be repeated with the clippers switched on, and only when the dog's natural alarm has subsided, should the trimming be started. The Puppy Clip is generally used for dogs under a year old. The foreface, muzzle and under the chin as far as the throat are clipped close. Always hold the dog's muzzle firmly shut while it is being clipped. The tail is trimmed except for a pom-pom on the end, and the feet are also clipped. The Lion, or English Saddle, Clip is the only acceptable one in the breed ring for adult dogs. This elaborate style has the face, feet and tail clipped as for the Puppy Clip. A mane of hair is left over the forequarters as far back as the last rib, and the hair on the haunches is shortened to about three-quarters of an inch in length. Bracelets of hair are left around the ankle joints on the front legs, and the ankle and stifle joints on the back legs.

93

Yorkshire Terrier

Irish Water Spaniels, American Water Spaniels and Curly-coated Retrievers are three extraordinary breeds whose coats are required to have either tight ringlets or crisp curls. They should be brushed hard with a stiff, bristled brush to remove tangles. Wetting encourages the formation of the oily ringlets, so the spaniels can be sprinkled lightly after grooming and allowed to dry.

When handling toy breeds it should be remembered that they need very gentle handling and grooming tools scaled to their size if possible. Care must be taken that they do not have an opportunity to jump from the grooming table, and a non-slip rubber mat will give them a greater sense of security when being bathed.

The glorious coat of the Pekinese, for example, is maintained by brushing and more brushing with the right kind of brush. This should have bristles about an inch or so in length, set in a rubber pad. Cleansing powder or a damp chamois leather are all that are used to remove any dirt. Great care must be taken to protect the eyes from injury, as breeds with protruding eyes are prone to eye ulcers after even a slight scratch.

The coat of the Maltese should be straight and of a silky texture. A soft, bristle brush is needed, and the pure white color necessitates a lot of bathing. Some breeders prefer to lather the dog in the style of a barber about to give a shave, rather than to stand the animal in a sink of water.

The Yorkshire Terrier probably has more emphasis placed on the color, texture and length of its coat than any other show breed. Though the only trimming necessary is to neaten the fringes around the feet, the care of the coat is a complicated business. The right brushes are difficult to find. They should have softish bristles, up to two or three inches in length. The hair is parted from the tip of the nose to the root of the tail, as it is in the Maltese. It is then brushed so that it hangs as flat and straight as possible. Ideally, the coat should reach the ground, including the mustache and cheek hair. In order to protect the hair and prevent the ends from splitting, it is divided into locks, each of which is rolled up into a piece of soft material or tissue paper and secured with a rubber band, between shows.

Maltese

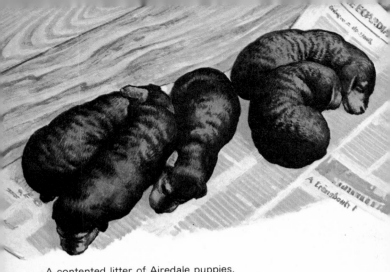

A contented litter of Airedale puppies.

BREEDING DOGS

There is a moral in the fact that very few dealers, buying and selling quantities of puppies, ever bother to breed their own stock. Few people make money out of breeding dogs. These include a few kennels with a high reputation and also the unscrupulous who use bitches as breeding machines. Most people take it up as a satisfying hobby because they are interested in showing and want to breed something better.

It is tempting, when considering the selling price of a litter of six or eight pups, to be misled as to the profit. Even if you are breeding from a pet bitch and do not wish to weigh the cost of her keep and the labor involved, the stud fee, possible veterinary bills and the rearing of the puppies to a marketable age, plus the cost of advertising, will come to a formidable total. If you are keeping a number of dogs, capital outlay on kennels and their subsequent depreciation will have to be added to a debit list which will also include rates or taxes, show entries and transport, labor and food bills, and also the expenses of a veterinary surgeon.

Many people start breeding with a bitch they already own. This may not always be the wisest move if you are interested

in producing show-quality puppies. If you have a poor quality bitch with a number of outstanding faults, it will be cheaper in the long run not to breed her but to start with a better foundation animal. Ideally this would be a bitch who has had a litter, and who, though she may not have a long string of show successes herself, comes from a line of high quality, containing many show winners. Unfortunately few such animals come on the market, as most kennel owners are only too well aware of the value of a good breed bitch. It is more likely that you will have to start with a bitch puppy. Here again it is better to choose an animal with sound typical ancestry on both the sire and the dam's side, than one sired by an outstanding dog out of an indifferent bitch. If possible the fertility of the line the puppy comes from should also be taken into account, though this information may be difficult to obtain.

The pedigree of a purebred animal, being merely a list of names, is of limited value. What is valuable is knowledge of the individuals mentioned. Very long pedigrees are really only of historical interest. It is of more practical use to have extensive knowledge of the characteristics of parents, grandparents and great-grandparents. When breeding dogs, health and temperament should have as much importance as conformation. The majority of puppies from any kennel are sold to pet homes, and their owners will value the health and good nature of their pet far more than the exact shape of the eye or color of the toenails. Useful information, then, should include an assessment of temperament, such details about the dog's health as can be obtained (including the sire's and dam's age at death and the cause of same), as well as a list of breed faults and virtues. Many well-established and successful breeders carry this information in their heads, but a card index is a more reliable method. Records of litter brothers and sisters will enable you to broaden the spectrum and get a clearer picture of the qualities your dog will be

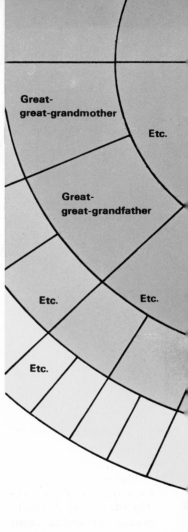

Example of a pedigree set out in a wheel formation.

likely to have inherited and to pass on to her offspring.

This type of record-keeping should form part of the personal dossier of every dog used in your breeding program. The file should also include pedigree, registration card, dog license, inoculation certificate, details of show wins and a breeding record. This record should give the date of the bitch's seasons, when she was mated and to whom, mention of anything unusual at the whelping, and sex, color markings and quality of the puppies. A good photograph could also be included.

Two complementary methods of fixing type in a kennel are widely used, line-breeding and inbreeding. In fact, they are different degrees of the practice of mating together animals that are related to each other. Line-breeding to an outstanding dog means breeding animals in whose pedigree that individual appears repeatedly both on the sire's and dam's side. It is, of course, perfectly possible to line-breed to several individuals at once. Inbreeding is an intensification of the process, using father-to-daughter or brother-to-sister matings. This has the effect of reducing the inherited variables and fixing both the good and bad qualities to a high degree. Anyone who inbreeds must be prepared to cull ruthlessly any results that do not measure up to the required high standard. A skillful breeder using unrelated foundation stock will, in a few generations, produce a type of family likeness that can be recognized at a glance by the knowledgeable.

Although a detailed knowledge of genetics is not essential, everyone who breeds dogs will find it helpful to understand

Diagram showing how X is line-bred to Y.

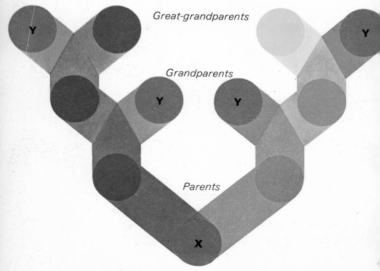

Great-grandparents

Grandparents

Parents

some of the terms used. The basic unit of inheritance is the gene. These can be described as coded chemical computers, dictating the potential of development of a new individual in every aspect. The genes are arranged in strings called chromosomes. Each species of animal has a characteristic number of chromosomes present in the nucleus of each cell, and the dog has 39 pairs. A division in the nucleus of the reproductive cells ensures that only one of each pair of chromosomes is contained in the egg or the sperm when it is formed. Therefore when an egg is fertilized by a sperm uniting with it, the original number of chromosomes is restored, half coming from the reproductive cell of the mother and half from the father. The genetic make-up of an animal is called the genotype and is of primary importance to a dog breeder. The phenotype is the label for the physical characteristics of the animal as a whole, and is of primary importance to the exhibitor. As the phenotype can obviously be altered by anything from feeding to surgery, it does not always provide reliable clues to the animal's genotype.

Example of color breeding in Dachshunds.

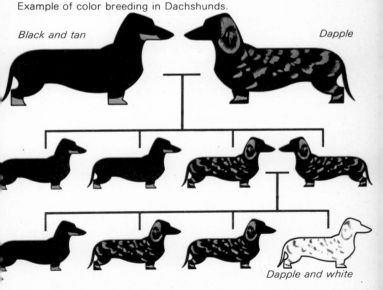

Black and tan

Dapple

Dapple and white

Diagram 1

The genes are believed to be arranged on the chromosomes in a definite order, and corresponding genes in the same place on a pair of chromosomes affect the same characteristics. The Mendelian theory, one of the foundation stones of the comparatively recent science of genetics, states that one of the two genes can be more powerful or assertive (i.e., 'dominant') and mask the effect of the other, the 'recessive'. A simple example will show how the statistical odds of an offspring inheriting a particular characteristic from its parents can be worked out. If father has a dark coat and the gene for this characteristic is dominant, his genetic make-up may consist of two dominant genes for a dark coat, or one dominant gene for a dark coat masking the effects of the other recessive gene for a light coat. If mother has a light coat she must have two recessive genes, and the dominant gene which would mask the light coat must be absent. The puppies from such parents would all be dark-coated if the father has two dominant genes for this characteristic (see Diagram 1). If the father carries a hidden recessive gene for a light coat, half the puppies will be light-coated and

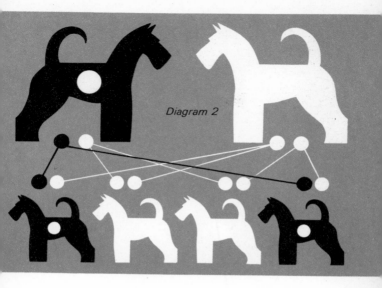

Diagram 2

half will be dark (see Diagram 2). It must be remembered that these odds will only apply where the numbers of offspring are large enough to be statistically significant.

Unfortunately for dog breeders it is now recognized that this simple pattern only occurs in a few cases. It is of value, for instance, in some forms of color breeding. Not many genes act independently in the manner suggested by Mendel. Most of the characteristics that dog breeders are interested in producing are the result of the reactions of a number of genes (i.e., they are polygenic). Again not all animals carrying a dominant gene for a particular feature will show the characteristic associated with that gene. The climate of the other genes may effect the outcome, modifying the result or changing it completely. Where a dominant gene does not always manifest itself in an animal carrying it, the percentage of individuals that do show it is the measure of the gene's penetrance. In the examples given in the diagrams above and on preceding pages, all genes are assumed to have 100 percent penetrance.

A St. Bernard showing symptoms of entropion.

No inherited abnormalities are peculiar to purebred stock, but their elimination is the concern of all serious dog breeders and the veterinary profession. The spread of such inherited defects through a breed may occur in a number of ways, one of the most usual being that a widely used and popular stud dog is carrying a recessive gene for such a defect. Interbreeding among his descendants will eventually bring the abnormality to light—and if he was a fashionable and prolific sire, the numbers affected can be quite large. To rid a breed of any inherited defect is a slow and difficult business. In many cases the exact mode of inheritance is not yet understood, in others the affliction cannot be detected until relatively late in the animal's life, perhaps after its breeding career is over. The following list gives the more important anomalies.

Hip Dysplasia—a malformation of the hip joint. Possibly the most widespread defect and discussed at length on page 144.

Patella Luxation—a deformity of the knee joint where the kneecap slips out of the groove laid down for it in the thigh-bone. Severe cases cannot walk. The condition can sometimes be corrected by surgery. Toy and miniature breeds are particularly affected. The exact mode of inheritance is unknown but it is believed to be polygenic.

Progressive Retinal Atrophy—a deterioration in sight leading to total blindness. There are at least two different forms of this, inherited differently in different breeds. Unfortunately early diagnosis is not yet possible and identification of P.R.A. needs expert specialist examination. In some breeds dogs cannot be pronounced clear of the defect before they are past the age of breeding.

Cryptorchidism—failure of one or both testes to descend into the scrotum. The method of inheritance is uncertain but probably polygenic. The American and English Kennel Clubs have banned the exhibition of cryptorchids.

Entropion—inversion of the eyelids causing constant irritation and watering of the eye. This is possibly due to a dominant gene with incomplete penetrance. Minor surgery will relieve the condition. The American Kennel Club has banned the exhibition of dogs with this defect.

Bad cases of Hip Dysplasia will have wasted hind-quarters.

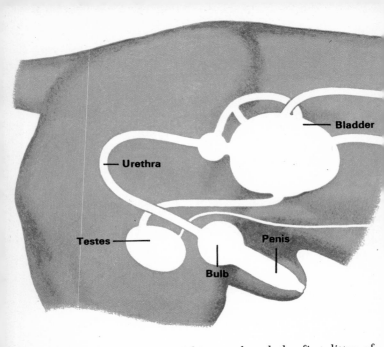

For a novice owner wishing to breed the first litter of puppies, the choice of a sire may seem difficult. If your bitch has come from a well-established kennel, her breeder's advice can be sought as to the most suitable dog. Where this is not possible, the dog magazines carry advertisements of dogs standing at stud, giving details of addresses and fees. The strong points of the dog should, if possible, be the very qualities in which your bitch is weak. What is not advisable is to follow the line of reasoning that suggests mating a short-backed bitch to a long-backed dog with the hope of getting a litter of medium-backed puppies. The result is more likely to be a mixture of long- and short-backed puppies than the desirable mean. In a litter sired by a dog with the correct length of back, you will be more likely to find the majority of puppies taking after their father.

Bitches vary tremendously in the frequency with which they come into season or on heat. A six-monthly estrus cycle is most usual, but with many bitches the interval is

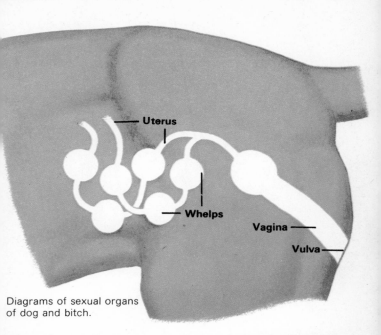

Uterus

Whelps

Vagina

Vulva

Diagrams of sexual organs
of dog and bitch.

longer, and with a few it is slightly shorter. If the interval is
very much shorter there is possibly some hormone imbalance
that needs veterinary attention. The first season can occur at
any age from six to eighteen months. No bitch should be
mated until her own growth is complete, and this generally
means before her second or, in the case of a late-maturing
breed, her third season. Conversely it is not wise to breed a
maiden bitch for the first time if she is over the age of five
years, though fit and healthy matrons may well have successful litters past this age. Wild dogs come into estrus once a
year and though one of the effects of domesticity has been to
increase the frequency in the domestic animal, it is inhumane
to breed from a bitch at her every season. A litter a year is
better both for the health of the bitch and the vigor of the
puppies. The only exception might be where a small litter
has been reared with little strain to the mother. In this case
she might be mated again at her next season before being
rested for a year.

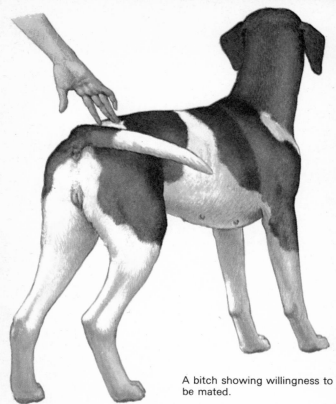

A bitch showing willingness to be mated.

The care of a bitch in season demands constant vigilance if a misalliance is to be avoided. She should always be exercised on the lead, as even a normally obedient animal may run off in order to follow her sexual instincts. As her odor is attractive to dogs, a course of veterinary chlorophyll will reduce the liklihood of unwanted attentions. Alternatively, sponging her hindquarters with a deodorizing fluid, or masking her scent with one of the aerosol sprays sold for this purpose, helps to prevent dogs paying her so much attention. A bitch will urinate more frequently when she is in season, and this will enable suitors to track her to her door. Carrying her or taking her by car for the first few hundred yards from home helps to break the trail. Dogs are liable to show unexpected agility and resourcefulness in reaching a sexually attractive bitch, so she should not be left unwatched unless shut in the house, kennel or roofed run.

Spaying (i.e., removing the ovaries) is one method of dealing with the nuisance of having to confine a bitch for six weeks of the year. Guide dogs for the blind are usually spayed bitches, and it is recognized that there are few bad side effects, provided the operation takes place after the animal is sexually mature. No spayed bitches can be exhibited and, as the operation is a major one, a period of careful nursing is required afterward.

Even after mating, a bitch needs supervision until the end of her season, as she may be quite willing to accept a number of dogs as mates. Should a misalliance take place, the unwanted pregnancy can be terminated by a veterinary surgeon within 48 hours of the mating. There can be dangerous side effects, and you may be advised to allow the bitch to have the litter. It is not true that a mongrel litter will ruin a purebred bitch's breeding career. Subsequent litters with pedigree sires will in no way be affected.

The owner of the stud dog should be contacted as soon as the bitch comes into season, and he will probably suggest the best day for the mating to take place. In most cases this will be the twelfth day or so from the first sign of a blood-stained discharge from the vulva. However, many bitches do not work to rule, and successful matings have been recorded from the third to the twenty-fifth day. The signs to be watched for which indicate the bitch's readiness to mate are a typical stance with tail twisted to one side and the vulva very prominent. This will be very considerably swollen with a moist, flaccid appearance. The blood-stained discharge will have ceased and been replaced by one of a yellowish color. Many stud dog owners are prepared to board visiting bitches for a day or two in order to make completely sure that the mating takes place at the right time.

Artificial insemination, though it has been carried out successfully, has not yet reached the foolproof stage of being a practical proposition. Any experiments in this direction need prior permission from the appropriate Kennel Club if the progeny are to be registered as purebred.

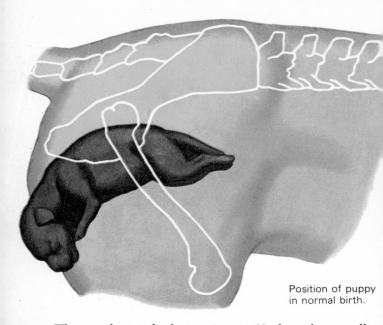

Position of puppy in normal birth.

The usual period of gestation is 63 days, but smaller breeds tend to whelp slightly earlier than larger ones. The puppies may be felt in the uterus by an expert between the 24th and 30th day of pregnancy, and after the fiftieth day x-ray diagnosis is also possible.

The in-whelp bitch should be kept as fit as possible with exercise. Worming should be carried out between the second and third week. Vitamins and a mineral supplement such as sterilized boneflour should be added to the diet. For the last three weeks the bitch should be accustomed to her whelping box and quarters. Newspaper makes a cheap, easily replaceable bedding. Some form of warmth is advisable during the first three weeks at least, and is best provided by an infra-red lamp suspended over the box.

The most reliable sign that whelping is imminent is a drop in the bitch's temperature from the normal 101.5° to about 99° or 98°. She will appear restless, lose her appetite and may

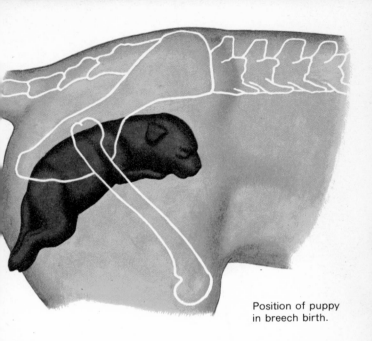

Position of puppy
in breech birth.

make a bed by tearing up the paper. Someone whom the bitch knows and trusts should stay with her throughout.

Puppies are normally born head first, encased in a membrane and with the umbilical cord still attached. The bitch will instinctively break the membrane, allowing the puppy to breathe, lick it vigorously to stimulate it and nip through the umbilical cord. Apparently lifeless puppies can often be revived by warmth, rubbing with a rough towel and artificial respiration. The afterbirth is expelled sometime after each birth and is usually eaten by the bitch. If contractions continue for more than three hours without a puppy being born, veterinary advice should be obtained. Advice should also be obtained if the puppies are more than three days overdue. Bitches sometimes have difficulty in expelling breech births (i.e., where the pup is tail first) or extra-large pups, and if these become stranded half-way out, they should be gripped with a piece of toweling and pulled outward and downward in time with the bitch's contractions.

111

A new-born litter of contented St. Bernard puppies.

The birth of a normal litter may take anything from two to twenty hours, and provided the bitch is resting quietly between contractions, no anxiety need be felt. When everything is over, the mother should be offered a milky drink and left to rest. During the next few days the mother's temperature should be watched to see that it returns to normal. Constant crying from the puppies indicates that something is wrong, as a warm, well-fed litter of young puppies makes little noise. The number in a litter varies tremendously, and eight is the maximum any bitch should be expected to rear unaided.

At three days old the puppies should be examined and their dew claws removed with sterilized scissors, if necessary. The breed standard should be consulted, as in some breeds it

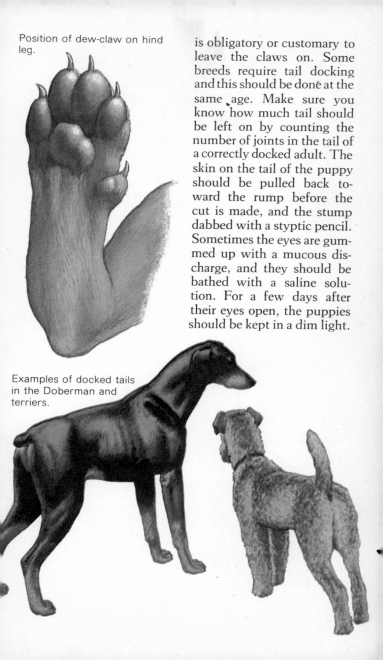

Position of dew-claw on hind leg.

is obligatory or customary to leave the claws on. Some breeds require tail docking and this should be done at the same age. Make sure you know how much tail should be left on by counting the number of joints in the tail of a correctly docked adult. The skin on the tail of the puppy should be pulled back toward the rump before the cut is made, and the stump dabbed with a styptic pencil. Sometimes the eyes are gummed up with a mucous discharge, and they should be bathed with a saline solution. For a few days after their eyes open, the puppies should be kept in a dim light.

Examples of docked tails in the Doberman and terriers.

In the United States, the ears of Boston Terriers, Bouviers des Flandres, Boxers, Brussels Griffons, Doberman Pinschers, Great Danes, Manchester Terriers and Schnauzers are customarily cropped. The operation should be performed by a qualified person when the puppies are between two and three months old. This is illegal in Great Britain.

Most young puppies are affected by roundworms, the eggs of which are able to pass via the blood stream of the bitch through the placenta into the fetus. A badly infested litter will appear pot-bellied and emaciated, while having voracious appetites. In such a case worming can be carried out as early as three weeks old, provided the right preparation is used. It is more usual to wait until the puppies are six weeks old, worming them once then and again ten days later. Reliable tablets are marketed for this purpose, and the instructions on the packet should be followed carefully.

Weaning should start at three weeks and be a slow and

Boxer with uncropped and cropped ears.

gradual process. A milk meal should be offered while the bitch is not present. This is best prepared from one of the dried milk powders formulated for puppies. If these are not available, cow's milk, slightly thickened with baby cereal, or, better still, goat's milk can be used. The meal should be offered lukewarm and the puppies' muzzles gently pushed in the pan. Most puppies take little time to learn to lap, and the milk meal can be offered twice a day until four weeks of age, when a third meal of scraped or ground raw meat should be introduced. Vitamins A and D and extra calcium should also be given and, if possible, the puppies should be fed separately to ensure that each gets a fair share. By five to six weeks, the meals should be increased from four to five, the secret of success being to give small meals at frequent intervals. Half the meals should be of meat and the others of milk thickened with cereal and then puppy meal. The puppies should also be allowed to feed from the mother, while she will let them.

Learning to eat from a bowl can be a messy experience.

Pekinese puppies ready for new homes.

Puppies are usually sold no earlier than eight weeks and should be advertised shortly before they are ready to leave. It is false economy to stint the advertising and be left with part of the litter, whose care and food bills will come to far more than an extra public announcement. The wording of the advertisement should not be misleading. No young puppy can be described with truth as a 'certain future champion'. Well-bred puppies of likely show quality should be advertised in periodicals likely to be read by fellow exhibitors, who will be interested in details of the breeding and so on. Pet stock is often better sold locally with breed descriptions rather than breeding details. Pedigree, registration card, diet sheet and inoculation details should be given to the purchaser.

Very long, unaccompanied journeys should be avoided for young puppies if possible. If this cannot be avoided, two puppies will travel together better than one. Any traveling box should be strong and light-weight with adequate ventilation holes placed where they will not cause a draft. A peaked roof will prevent freight being piled on top of the box, and battens under the floor of the box will keep it off cold, damp surfaces. Lifting handles on the outside and adequate labeling securely fastened to the box will both help railroad or airline staff. The door should have a wire mesh panel and a fastening that can be opened in an emergency but is not likely to be tampered with by mischievous passersby. The size of a box for an adult dog should be as follows: Height should enable the dog to stand upright without touching the roof; width should be twice that across the shoulder blades; length should be that of the dog when it is lying down, measured from the root of the tail to the outstretched forepaws.

Before exporting, the import regulations of the country of destination should be studied.

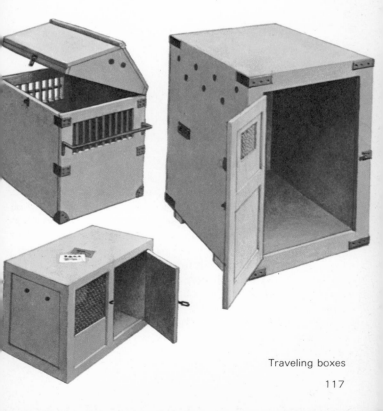

Traveling boxes

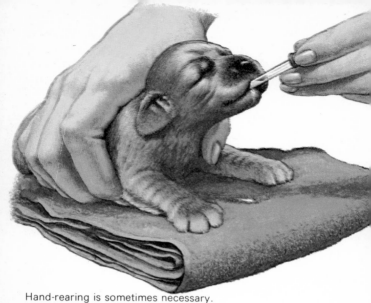

Hand-rearing is sometimes necessary.

Anyone left with orphan puppies should make every effort to find and introduce them to a foster mother rather than undertake hand-rearing. Puppies being introduced to a strange bitch should have some of her milk smeared on them to make them smell more familiar. Cats often make good foster mothers for the smaller breeds.

When hand-rearing is unavoidable the following formula can be used: 28 fluid ounces cow's milk, 7 fluid ounces light cream, 1 egg yolk, 1½ teaspoonfuls of sterilized bone meal and 1 teaspoonful of citric acid powder. This mixture can be made up and kept in the refrigerator, enough for each meal being heated up to body temperature. There are several commercial substitutes for bitch's milk which are excellent. The puppies will need to be fed every three or four hours throughout the day and night for the first week. During the second week the night feedings may gradually be reduced, until by the fourteenth day a late meal in the evening and an early one in the morning should be sufficient.

Methods of feeding, depending upon the size of the puppies, include eye droppers, dolls or premature babies' feeding bottles and the feeding tube. This last, once mastered, has the advantage that it is quicker and there is no possibility of the puppy inhaling the feed. You need a plastic hypodermic syringe and a flexible plastic tube of a suitable size to pass down the puppy's throat to the stomach. The tube is attached to the syringe, the necessary food is drawn up and the end of the tube is passed over the back of the animal's tongue and down the gullet into the stomach. All the utensils used should be sterilized in the same way as a baby's bottle between feedings. Each puppy should have a separate bed to prevent them sucking each others' tails and so on. The temperature for the first week should be kept at 85°, dropping to 80° in the second week and being progressively lowered to 70° by the end of the fourth week. After each feed the puppy's abdomen must be gently massaged with cotton wool dipped in olive oil in order to stimulate urination and defecation. As such puppies will not have received the protection of the antibodies present in their mother's milk, they must be immunized against distemper exceptionally early.

A bitch licks her puppies to encourage elimination.

Keeping a stud dog can be a profitable business provided there is sufficient demand for his services. This will depend to a large extent on his breeding and the number of show wins to his credit. A dog whose progeny are also winning in the ring will be even more in demand.

The management of a stud dog requires some understanding. The preliminaries and the speed with which mating takes place are extremely variable and knowledge of your own dog's peculiarities is your best guide as to management. In a normal mating where both dog and bitch are experienced, the bitch, if she is at the correct stage of estrus, will stand quietly with tail drawn to one side while the dog mounts. The dog will penetrate between the lips of the vulva giving a series of thrusting movements, during which the outer sheath of the penis is pushed right back and ejaculation takes place. The bulb of the penis becomes greatly enlarged and is prevented from slipping out of the bitch by the constrictor muscles of the vagina. It is this which constitutes the 'tie', which may last from five to thirty minutes or even longer. At this

Mounting

stage the male will usually dismount and turn himself completely around by lifting one hind leg over the bitch. This leaves the two animals standing facing in opposite directions, with rumps pressed together, and they will remain like this until the penis returns to its normal size and slips out. A 'tie' does not always occur, and this does not necessarily mean the mating will be unsuccessful.

A young dog is usually allowed to mate his first bitch when he is about ten months of age. This first service should be to a cooperative experienced bitch whose willingness will give the young dog confidence. Even if the bitch will stand quietly she should be held so that the dog gets used to assistance and is not put off by it when more difficult bitches are encountered.

Difficulties in mating can occur with a timid, under-sexed dog who will require a lot of encouragement, verbal and physical, and a nervous or ill-tempered bitch who is best muzzled and held. It is always easier if there are two assistants present at the time.

Position during the tie

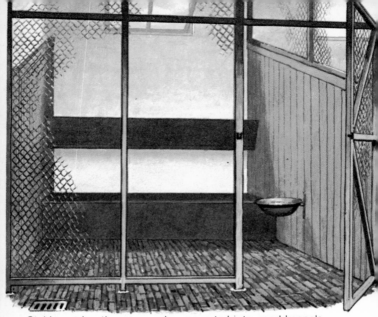
Stables and outhouses can be converted into good kennels.

KENNEL MANAGEMENT

Preoccupation with breeding and showing dogs often means that their number is likely to increase over the years with housing and kenneling tending to be a haphazard afterthought. Two aspects of keeping a number of dogs deserve more thought than is often given to them. One is that the general level of health of your stock depends a great deal on their housing. The second is that the design of such housing can do a great deal to reduce the time and labor of routine care. Even if existing outbuildings are adapted, these considerations still apply.

The basic requirement of any kennel is that it should be weatherproof. Ideally this means not only watertight and windproof, but also insulated against extremes of temperature. These features must be combined with adequate ventilation and natural lighting. The size must allow the dog to stand up and lie down in comfort. This size is a minimum.

As the dog is a gregarious animal it is often better to kennel two or three together, though with aggressive breeds or opinionated stud dogs this is not always possible. The larger kennel, too, is more easily cleaned out and, with this in mind, small kennels should be designed with a door occupying all of one end. Though wood is the traditional material for both commercially available and home-built kennels, it has a number of disadvantages. Being absorbent, both the outside and inside surfaces need regular coatings, preferably of lead-free paint or a polyurethane varnish. Door sills and other projections need protecting with sheet metal as many young dogs are destructive. Where the floor is concrete or the kennel is large, some form of wooden bed raised from the floor should be provided.

With toy dogs, indoor kennels are usually used. These can be built in tiers, like rabbit hutches, with removable metal trays to facilitate cleaning. As with any sort of kenneling arrangement, no dog should spend the entire time shut in.

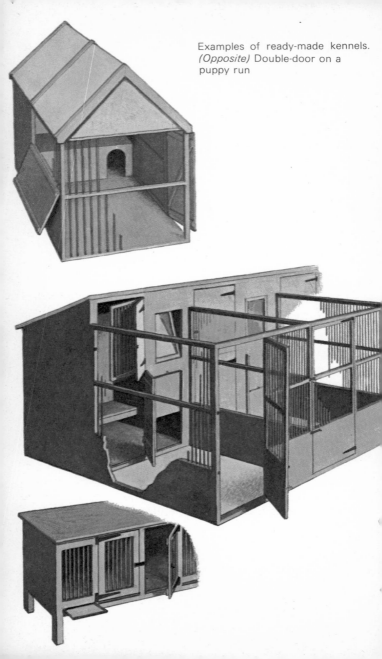

Examples of ready-made kennels.
(Opposite) Double-door on a puppy run

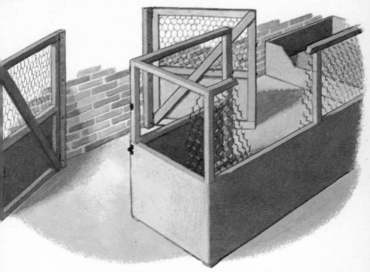

Kennels should be sheltered from the prevailing wind and laced so that the dogs get the maximum sun, while also having somewhere to retire into the shade. Kennel runs should be as large as possible, again housing more than one dog. Suggested minimal sizes might be 25 feet by 15 feet for two Great Danes, 8 feet by 20 feet for Alsatians or German Shepherds, and 2 feet by 4 feet for two Chihuahuas. The height of the fencing will obviously vary according to the breed housed. Most actively built, medium-sized breeds can clear six feet if they really want to, but few are impelled to make the attempt. Runs to accommodate bitches in season should be roofed for safety and placed out of sound or scent of the other kennels.

Grass or earth runs are not very satisfactory as they are difficult to keep clean. The kind of surface found on hard tennis courts is probably nearest the ideal, but most people have to be content with concrete. This should be laid with a definite slope down to a gutter so that water cannot collect and hosing down is easy. Some form of wooden platform should be provided for the dogs to lie on.

From the time-saving point of view it is an advantage to be able to open the kennel door from outside the run. All

125

doors should have catches which will snap shut when the door is slammed. With large dogs, a small sliding panel at the bottom of the run door will enable food and water dishes to be changed from the outside. For a puppy run, a double door or porch will prevent puppies dashing into the open every time someone attends to them. A trolley of some sort is invaluable for carrying numbers of food dishes, water and cleaning materials.

Kennel heating is a factor which must depend a great deal on the climate, situation and the breed in question. With a heavy-coated animal, kennel heating is unlikely to be necessary, provided the dog has a bed to retire to with some sort of roof. A box that is just big enough for the dog to stand up in will trap enough body heat for a long-coated dog to remain comfortable in the most severe weather. The food ration should be increased in the winter months, with a greater proportion of fat in the diet. This is, in effect, the fuel the dog will need to keep itself warm. Bedding should also be increased. Wheat straw is probably the material most com-

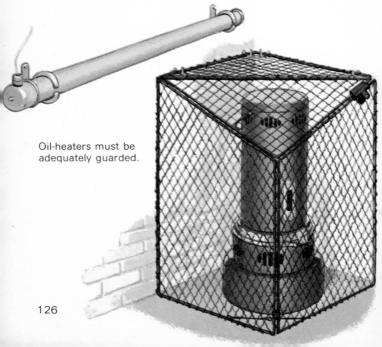

Oil-heaters must be adequately guarded.

Sleeping bed

monly used. Care should be taken to ensure that it is dry before being supplied to the dogs, and the bedding should be shaken out daily. As soon as it starts to break up it should be replaced. Hay is not a suitable bedding. It is dusty, full of irritating grass seeds, and is likely to harbor vermin. Excelsior woodwool has the advantages of cleanliness and warmth, but the strands of this tend to be tough and puppies and very small breeds can get inextricably tangled. Blankets do not provide the same warmth as bedding, which the dog can burrow into, and they require frequent cleaning.

A range of kennels under the same roof can often be heated economically by a boiler or solid fuel stove. Where electricity is available, tubular heaters hung out of the dog's reach are another possibility. Stoves, hot pipes and electrical wiring must be adequately guarded. Oil heating with paraffin stoves is in wide use because it is cheap. It is false economy to use antiquated heaters because they increase the risk of fires. All such heaters must be cleaned and maintained regularly. They are better fastened in position, so that they cannot be accidentally knocked over, and they should be surrounded by a nursery-type fire guard which covers the top as well as the sides.

The disposal of kennel waste will depend largely on the kennel size and locality. Where a few dogs are kept in urban surroundings, feces can be disposed of via the main sewage system. Alternatively, a dustbin with a well-fitting lid and containing the type of fluid used in chemical toilets can be used for the droppings. The chemical will prevent flies and smell, and the contents can be buried when the bin is full. Where there are no nearby neighbors and sawdust or straw form part of the waste, an incinerator will solve the problem. Another solution is a compost heap which will also incorporate household waste and gardening rubbish. Peat makes a good deodorizing substance for covering each layer daily. A pit in which the daily waste is covered with lime has also been successful.

Where large numbers of dogs are kept or handled, an isolation kennel is a necessity. In smaller establishments it is still a desirable feature, even if, for reasons of space, it has to be used for other purposes when not housing a sick

Incinerators are useful for the disposal of waste.

128

animal. Any dog that appears to be sick can be immediately segregated until an accurate diagnosis is made. Any such quarters must have heating and lighting and be as far from the other kennels as practicable. A sick animal should have its own feeding utensils, and the canine nurse must remember that clothing and footwear as well as hands will carry infection. A lab coat and boots, which can be dunked in disinfectant, can be left outside the kennel when not in use and will cut down the risk. Dogs are very susceptible to carbolic poisoning and for this reason the carbolic group of disinfectants should be avoided. Where thorough disinfecting is necessary and the building material permits it, a blowtorch flamed over the walls and floor is effective. In wooden kennels washing with disinfectant solution should be followed by allowing the kennel to air and dry for at least 14 days. If the kennel can be sealed up a fumigating candle can be used.

Whelping kennels also need heat and artificial light, as most bitches seem to give

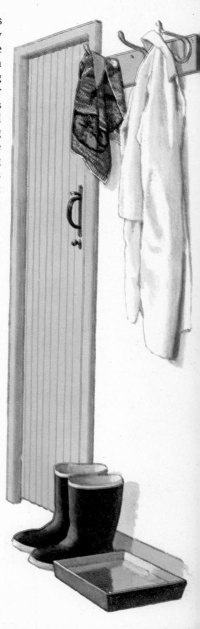

A change of clothing is needed for the sick room.

birth in the early morning hours. As puppies are born without an efficient heat regulating mechanism, they depend on warmth from their dam and their surroundings. An infrared lamp suspended over the whelping box or some kind of insulated heating pad in the box itself, will cut puppy losses. It is a great advantage to have a whelping kennel within hearing distance.

A service area for the

Further cupboards in the service area should contain first-aid equipment and cleaning materials. A filing system for kennel records should also be installed.

whole kennels is often neglected as a luxury, when from the point of view of labor it is a sensible provision. Ideally this should contain a food store with hods or galvanized containers that are vermin-proof. A refrigerator is needed for the meat supply. The economics of a deep freeze should be considered as this can be a worthwhile investment in cutting costs. The food preparation area should have a sink where feed bowls can be washed, and some form of burner. A pressure cooker is of more use than saucepans.

A cupboard for grooming equipment can be housed under a grooming table. A strategically placed mirror will help when trimming and a stand may be useful for controlling excitable dogs. A spray attachment for the dog bath or sink will save time. There should be a towel rail for drying dish cloths, chamois leathers and towels. A wire pen outside, in which a fan heater can be placed, will ensure that dogs are completely dry before being returned to their kennels.

Bulk buying is an advantage in caring for a number of dogs, and that is why storage space is so necessary.

Pressure cooker

Unlike human beings, the dog does little chewing except when trying to dismember something too large and hard to be swallowed. Little saliva gets mixed with a dog's food, and nearly all the digestion takes place with the powerful gastric juices of the stomach. A half to two-thirds of an adult dog's diet should be meat or an equivalent high protein food. This is usually beef or horseflesh, and the rules for serving it given on page 20 should be observed. Pork is often too rich for dogs to digest. It can pass on certain parasites, so it should always be thoroughly cooked. The same will apply to rabbit, which must also be boned. It has been suggested that feeding a lot of flesh from caponized poultry will cause a lowering of fertility. Uncleaned paunches, lungs and intestines can sometimes be obtained and these are usually relished by dogs. Eggs should be lightly cooked as raw egg white is not only indigestible but also liable to absorb certain vitamins in the digestive tract. Fat of some sort should be included in the diet. Dogs can thrive on diets containing more than a quarter fat, but 1½ tablespoons to a pound of lean meat is about the regular mean. Liver and hearts are other excellent foods. However, they are likely to cause diarrhea and should be introduced gradually. This also applies to all major diet changes.

Carbohydrates, a source of energy, are usually provided in the form of dog biscuits or biscuit meal. Many large kennels like to soak biscuit meal in the gravy from the meat until it is moist and crumbly.

The list of trace elements needed to sustain life is long, and most occur naturally in a varied diet. Food should be lightly salted occasionally, and a dog that eats no bones or milk may benefit from small amounts of bone meal to provide calcium. Vitamins A and D are best provided for growing animals by cod liver oil or halibut oil. Vitamin B should be present in good quality biscuit made from wholemeal flour, but can be given as unextracted, dried brewer's yeast. The dog can synthesize its own vitamin C and will obtain vitamin E from the fats in the diet. Complete vitamin pills for dogs are also marketed in pellet form.

Self-feeding hopper

ANATOMY

All dogs from the Chihuahua to the Great Dane have the same bones jointed in the same ways and held together by the same muscle structure. Indeed the foreleg of the dog has corresponding bones to the human arm, and the dog's hindlimb parallels the human leg. The dog, with limbs adapted for running, has much less sideways mobility than a man, so that although the upper arm, or humerus, joins the shoulder blade with much the same socket in both, the dog's limb down to the elbow is held close to the rib cage with skin and muscle. The leg below the 'wrist' joint is known as the pastern. In the dog's hind limb, the stifle is the joint corresponding to our knee, and the hock is the ankle. But the dog walks on its fingers and toes.

The dog's walk is a four-time movement, while the trot, which is the gait usually assessed in the show ring, is essentially a two-time movement. The diagonal pairs of legs move together. Seen from the side this gait will show the length of stride, freedom of forward movement and propulsion of the

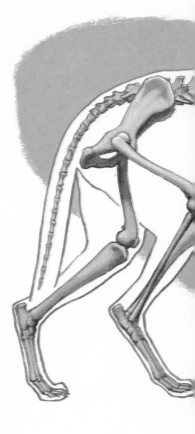

How the bones in the human forearm can be compared with those in the dog's front leg.

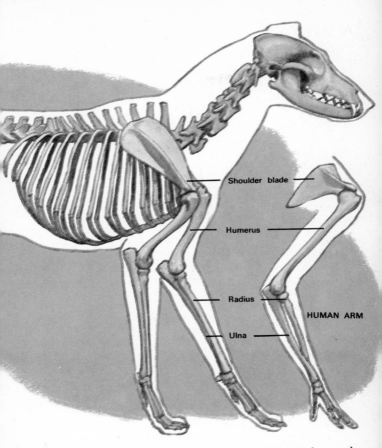

Shoulder blade

Humerus

Radius

Ulna

HUMAN ARM

limbs. Viewed with the dog coming toward the judge and then going away, the plane in which each limb travels in relation to the other can be assessed. Dogs can pace or amble, although this is a gait frowned on in the ring. It occurs when both legs on the same side of the body are moved together. The canter in the dog is the same as that of the horse with either one or the other front leg leading consistently. Most breeds extend this movement to the gallop, but Greyhounds and other fast breeds use a style which is really a series of enormous leaps to cover the ground.

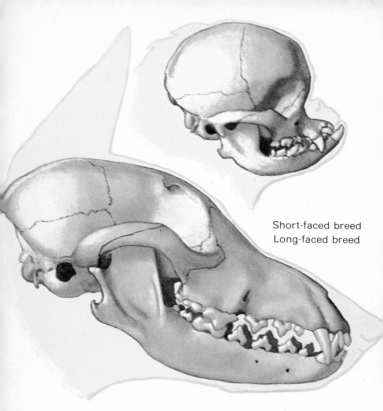

Short-faced breed
Long-faced breed

The chief difference between the skulls of a long-faced and a short-faced breed is not in the width of the cranium but in the length of the nasal bones. Short-faced breeds, such as Pekinese, therefore, have much reduced scenting powers and often have difficulty in breathing. The head is of great importance in many breeds, and breed standards are usually very explicit on this. Two terms often met with may need definition. The *occiput* is the bone that can be felt as a knob on the back of the skull. It is very prominent in some breeds such as Bloodhounds. The *stop* is the depression between the eyes at the junction of the nose and the skull. It is very pronounced in the short-faced breeds and non-existent in breeds like the Borzoi.

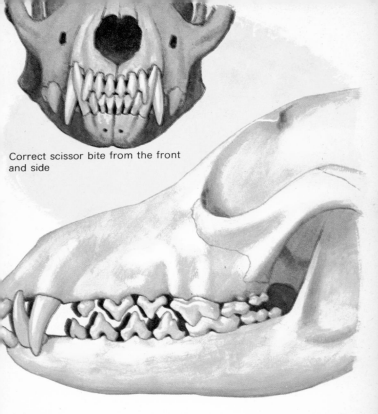

Correct scissor bite from the front and side

Most breeds are required to have a scissor bite where the front upper teeth just overlap the lower. A pincer bite where the upper and lower teeth meet level is also sometimes permissible. An undershot jaw where the lower teeth protrude some way in front of the upper is a fault in most breeds but a desired characteristic in some, such as the Bulldog. An overshot mouth where the upper jaw is the protruding one is a fault in all breeds. The first, temporary set of milk teeth are 28 in number. These should start appearing when a puppy is about three weeks old and should be all through by about the fifth or sixth week. These start to be replaced by the 42 permanent teeth, which the dog begins to get at about four months.

The upper jaw should have three incisors, one canine and six pre-molar and molar teeth on each side. The lower jaw is the same except for one extra molar at the back. In a number of breeds one or more of the cheek teeth are often missing.

There are six different patterns of ear carriage among purebred dogs, and some are more difficult to breed for than others. In an erect ear the cartilage must be strong enough to support the position when the muscles at the base pull it upright. The final ear carriage cannot be assessed in many breeds until the permanent teeth are all through. Possibly the most difficult ear type is the semi-prick ear found on

(*Top*) Pendent, prick, button, prick, rose, semi-prick.
(*Bottom*) Eye shape and position vary from breed to breed.

Collies and Shetland Sheepdogs, where only the tip of the ear is required to droop. Many puppies of these breeds have the tips of their ears weighted to encourage them to hang down.

Eye shape and position show just as much divergence as ear carriage. The shape of the eye is influenced not so much by the size of the eyeball as the shape and tension of the eyelids and the disposition of the fat around the bony socket of the eye in the skull. Breeds where the emphasis has been on small, slit eyes are more likely to have trouble from entropion. Many standards specify dark eyes as being desirable. Eye and coat color are related; lighter colored dogs have lighter colored eyes to match.

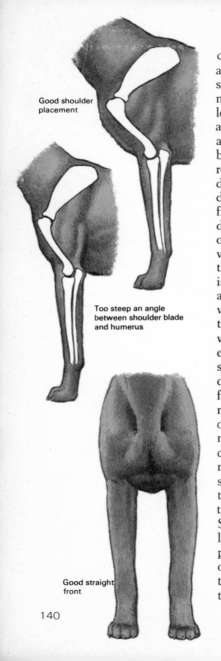

Good shoulder placement

Too steep an angle between shoulder blade and humerus

Good straight front

Each breed has its own characteristic movement and, as all dogs have basically the same bone structure, this must be due to the relative length of the bones and their angles in relation to one another. In many cases these breed differences can be related back to the work the dog was originally bred to do. Any propulsive thrust from any limb that is not directed solely along the line of travel is inefficient and wasteful of effort. In practice this means that when the dog is approaching, both forelegs are moving in parallel planes with no weakness shown by the elbows rotating outward, the pasterns turning either in or out, or the feet splaying sideways or paddling. Seen from the side the forward stride in most breeds must have reach and freedom of swing. The body should move forward smoothly. A chopping, swaying movement usually indicates unsoundness somewhere, although a few breeds specify that a slight roll is permissible. Seen from the rear the hindlimbs must show straight parallel action. The degree of propulsion is indicated by the flexing of the hocks and the whole pad of the foot being visible as the dog pushes off.

The front movement depends a great deal on the placement of the shoulder blade. The most efficient angle for this to be placed is at forty-five degrees to the ground. Where the humerus joins the shoulder blade at an angle of approximately ninety degrees, this allows the greatest freedom of reach for the forelegs. Many other factors come into play, one of which is the head and neck carriage. A dog with a fairly long neck held high not only looks better but is liable to move better as well. This is partly because some of the neck muscles play a part in the forward movement of the front legs and partly because length of neck and well-laid-back shoulders are often found together.

Most breeds are required to have either 'cat' feet or 'hare' feet. The difference between the two is in the length of the digital bones. The longer bones in the hare foot give greater leverage for speed but are more likely to be injured than those in the more compact cat foot. In both cases the toes should be held closely together and the pads well cushioned.

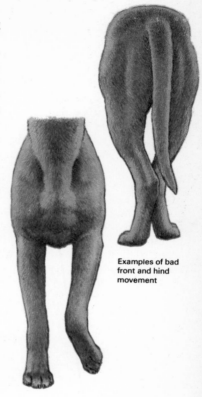

Examples of bad front and hind movement

Good front movement

The heart and lung room obviously has a great deal of effect on speed and stamina. The space for these organs within the rib cage depends more on its depth and length than on its width. Dogs with barrel ribs have not got a great deal more room for lung expansion than slab-sided ones. The ideal from this point of view is a deep brisket, a slightly pointed oval rather than a circle in cross section. This rib cage should extend a long way back without losing too much depth. The area between the end of the rib cage and the pelvis is the loin. This lumbar region carries muscles which help to lift the front of the dog at speed. Although a long, slack loin indicates weakness, too short a loin can cramp the hind action.

As with most mammals the straighter legs in the front carry the main weight while the more angulated hind legs provide the propulsion for movement. The drive is transmitted from the hind legs through the tilted pelvis to the spinal column. The straighter the line through which this propelling force is transmitted, the better. The power of the hind legs is achieved in part by their freedom to swing through

s large an arc as possible, and this means long thigh and
leg bones with the hocks well let down. These long bones,
accompanied by their long, powerful muscles, must be
well angulated or one of the results would be a dog whose
rump stood much higher than its withers. As well as the
angulation, the flexion of these joints must also be a consideration. Not all breeds are expected to produce speed. The
opposite extreme occurs in the Chow where, though the
hindlegs should be muscular and the hocks well let down,
the limb is required to be as straight as possible.

There is an even greater variety in tails than ears. Most
breeds are born with the characteristic breed tail shape.
Where faults come in is usually in tail carriage. The terrier
who is required to have a perky, upright tail may have it set too
low for it ever to reach the desired angle. On the other hand
the Dachshund, meant to carry its tail level with the back,
may well be waving it in an almost vertical position. As
the tail is a barometer to mental attitude, the nervous dog
is unlikely to carry its tail well.

143

Hip Dysplasia (H.D.) is a term which simply means abnormal development of the hip. This condition could have a number of causes, but it is the congenital and inherited defect of the hips which is causing most concern.

The hip joint is a ball and socket joint with the head of the femur or thigh bone fitting snugly into a socket in the pelvis. In the dog affected with H.D. these two bones do not fit together with the required degree of correlation. The deep cup of the socket is flattened, so that there is a varying amount of play between it and the femur head. In severe cases the hips are completely dislocated and the dog is crippled and in constant pain. In cases like this the condition can sometimes be relieved by surgery with the removal of the whole femur head. The dog compensates for this by abnormal muscle development and can move fairly normally without pain. Slight cases of H.D. cannot be detected by the dog's movement or behavior, although there will be arthritic development in the joint as the dog ages. The only method of diagnosis is by X-ray, and this must be done after the dog is a year old before it can be pronounced clear. Very accurate readings are required to detect any slight deviation from normal.

Normal hip   Malformed hip joint

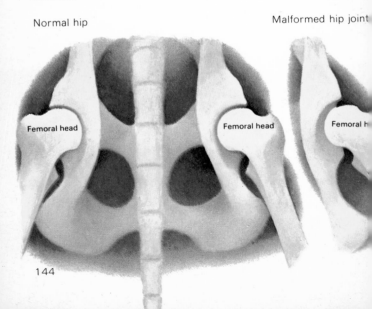

Femoral head   Femoral head   Femoral h

H.D. occurs in cats, horses and cattle and was first recorded in man over two thousand years ago. It was first diagnosed in dogs in 1935 and has since been shown to be widespread, occurring in most breeds of dog irrespective of their size. The mode of inheritance is not completely understood and, in view of the number of breeds involved, there may very well be more than one. Environment also plays a part as it has been shown that extra heavy or overweight puppies are more likely to develop abnormal hips.

As the condition is so widespread it is not possible to remove all the affected animals from the breeding stock. Even if this were possible it would only partially eliminate the disease, as radiologically clear parents can produce puppies with H.D., although the proportion of affected pups is much smaller. The only method of control is to upgrade one's kennel stock by a process of selection. Swedish research has shown that if one breeds from dogs with only slight defects, removing from the breeding stock any progeny worse than the parents, by the fourth generation no more gross clinical cases will appear. By this method, even if dog breeders cannot get rid of H. D., they will at least ensure that they breed no more cripples.

One of the measurements taken to detect hip dysplasia.

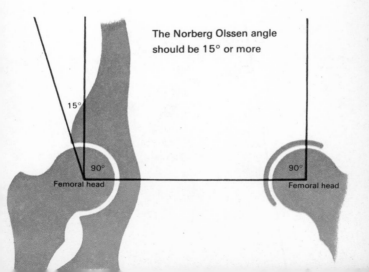

The Norberg Olssen angle
should be 15° or more

15°

90°
Femoral head

90°
Femoral head

Giving pills and liquid medicine

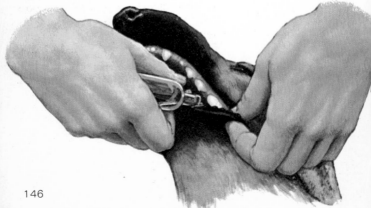

ILL HEALTH

Diagnosis and treatment of illness is the job of the veterinary surgeon, whose job is simplified if he is called at the outset, rather than when the dog is weakened and exhausted. Symptoms to be watched for are any sudden inexplicable changes of normal behavior, such as excessive drinking, sudden loss of appetite, continual vomiting or diarrhea, or unusual lethargy. Discharging or inflamed eyes, and rapid, shallow breathing or continued coughing can all be symptoms of something serious. If any of these are associated with a high temperature, often indicated by a hot, dry nose, or a very low temperature, then professional advice should be sought.

A dog's temperature is taken rectally and is normally 101.5° F. The only exception to this is the very rare, hairless breeds, whose normal temperature is one to two degrees higher. After strenuous activity or excitement a dog's temperature will have risen and will not be a reliable guide as to health. To take the temperature the dog must be firmly held to prevent it sitting down, and the end of the thermometer, smeared with vaseline, should be inserted into the rectum for about an inch. Any reading above 102.5° or below 100° should be regarded with suspicion.

Dosing with liquid medicine is best done with the dog in a sitting position. The correct dose of a liquid is given more easily if it is first placed in a small bottle rather than a spoon. The corner of the dog's lips should be pulled out making a pouch into which the medicine can be poured. Keep the mouth shut and the muzzle up, until by stroking the throat the dog is felt to have swallowed. Tablets or pills can sometimes be disguised in food. Otherwise the mouth should be opened and the pill placed as far down the throat as possible. Hold the mouth shut until the capsule has been swallowed. Some dogs become very clever at keeping pills under their tongues, so watch when you let go that your dog does not go into a corner and spit the offending article out. Powdered medicines can be shaken onto the tongue.

Nursing a sick dog requires calmness, kindness and a reassuring manner. Dogs are sensitive to tones of voice in people they know, and a worried manner is not helpful.

k dog needs warmth, quiet and cleanliness. If it must ~n out to relieve itself, it should have a coat that covers the chest and stomach as well as the back. A light diet will include easily digested foods such as milk dishes enriched with baby cereal and honey, white fish and white meat. A pat of butter or a smear of meat essence will sometimes persuade a reluctant dog to eat.

Ear troubles, often with widely differing causes, are very often lumped together under the name canker. Symptoms of ear troubles include constant scratching of the ear, an objectionable smell from the ear canal and a dog that continually shakes its head. Ears should be regularly inspected for signs of trouble, which can be caused by excessive wax, ear mites or a foreign body such as a grass seed. Until the trouble is accurately diagnosed treatment will be guesswork. Prevention includes making sure that the ears are always kept dry. Some breeds have excess hair in the ear canal and this should be removed by plucking as it collects dirt and wax and prevents air circulating and drying the canal. Although the inner flap of the ear can be cleaned with cotton soaked in olive oil, nothing should ever be inserted into the canal itself.

Dogs with eyes that are watering may have been lying in a draft or have some grit irritating the eyeball. In either of these cases, bathing the eye with a lukewarm saline solution will help (one teaspoonful of salt to one pint of water). Constant eye trouble may mean entropion and need veterinary help.

Rubbing the head on the ground can be a sign of ear trouble.

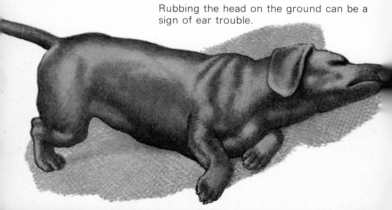

Investigate the cause of constant scratching.

A dog that is constantly scratching may have canker, fleas or a sore spot of some sort. It is not natural for a dog to scratch endlessly, and the cause should be looked for and eliminated. Sore or red skin should be soothed with calamine. If this does not help and a skin disease seems likely, then again an accurate diagnosis must be made before effective treatment can begin. It is useful to remember that if an ointment is applied immediately before taking the dog out, the excitement of the outing very often distracts it from trying to lick it off.

The dog has two marble-sized glands located on either side of the anus. The passage of the feces normally squeezes these anal glands sufficiently to empty them but modern feeding methods often mean the bowel movements are too soft to do this effectively. The result is that the glands become clogged with a foul-smelling secretion. As well as smelling obnoxious, the dog will drag his hindquarters along the ground and lick the anus. In neglected cases abscesses will form. The glands can be emptied by squeezing, a knack which should be learned by watching someone competent first.

Lameness through a small cut or sore pad should be treated by standing the foot in a bowl of disinfectant solution. Occasionally tar or paint may get stuck to the hair between the pads. This can be removed with olive oil or butter. On no account use paint remover which will inflame and irritate the skin. Sore, thin and tender pads can be hardened by painting with surgical alcohol. In snowy weather, breeds with a great deal of hair on their feet often become iced up with hard balls of snow and grit between the pads. A coat of vaseline beforehand will prevent this. Some dogs suffer from painful cysts between the toes. These need opening by a veterinarian who may advise poulticing first to bring them to a head.

Some dogs wearing plaster casts after an accident will take a delight in chewing them. Covering the cast with shiny insulating tape or painting it with mustard will sometimes deter them. Such a cast can be protected in wet weather by a plastic bag held on with a rubber band.

All puppies should be vaccinated against distemper, hepatitis and two forms of leptospirosis. Vaccines are produced which provide protection against all four of these diseases in the one dose. Distemper, and the variety of it known as hardpad, is an infectious virus disease whose symptoms include high temperature and discharges from the eyes and nose. This disease gives rise to nervous conditions, such as fits, caused by the infection of the brain by the virus. Treatment is difficult and the outcome is uncertain. Even if the dog recovers, permanent damage to the nervous system is likely.

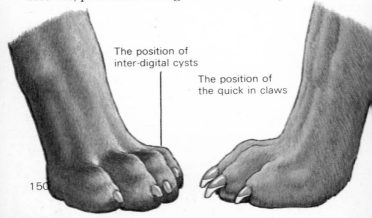

The position of inter-digital cysts

The position of the quick in claws

A large cardboard collar will prevent a dog from licking a wound

Contagious hepatitis is another infectious virus disease, which is liable to damage the liver. It is an acute illness which attacks the young in particular. The leptospiral infections, one of which is spread by rats and the other caught from the urine of 'carrier' dogs, cause fever and jaundice symptoms, attacking mainly the kidneys.

Puppies get the protection of their mother's antibodies passed on to them through the colostrum (i.e., the first milk produced after birth). These natural antibodies gradually disappear, but while they are still circulating in the puppies' bloodstream they inhibit any attempts at artificial vaccination. For this reason puppies are not usually inoculated until they are three months old, when it is calculated that the maternal antibodies will have disappeared. If circumstances make it advisable to inoculate before this age your veterinary

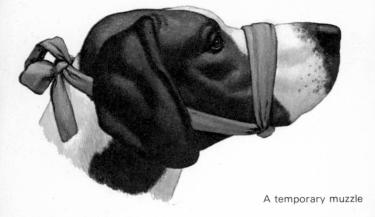

A temporary muzzle

surgeon may recommend a second dose shortly after the first. Hepatitis vaccination usually lasts a lifetime, but the distemper and leptospiral immunities will require booster doses.

Emergency first aid is most likely to be needed in the case of road accidents. Any dog in pain or severely frightened is likely to bite anyone within reach, so a muzzle should be fashioned from a tie or belt before the dog is helped. This emergency muzzle should be looped around the dog's mouth, tied under the chin and then tied again at the back of the neck. A badly injured dog should be carried on something rigid; a coat held taut between two people will do if nothing else can be utilized. Suspected fractures and broken limbs should also be held immobile until the dog can receive expert attention. Splints can be improvised from anything rigid. Bleeding can be temporarily stopped by a pad of material pressed firmly on the site of the wound.

Shock or collapse may occur after any severe pain or loss of blood. The dog may appear barely conscious, with staring eyes and shallow breathing. The lips, tongue and gums will be pale and the body cold. The dog should be kept warm with blankets and hot water bottles. Do not give anything by mouth until the animal has been seen by a vet.

If the dog is unconscious through asphyxia, the cause must first be removed. If the dog has choked, whatever is in

Artificial respiration

the throat must be either pulled out or pushed down. In drowning cases, some of the water must be removed from the lungs. A small enough dog can be picked up by the hind legs and shaken or swung. Where coal gas poisoning has occurred, fresh air is essential. A dog may also be unconscious through electric shock. It is essential to make sure the electricity is turned off before touching the animal. Artificial respiration should be tried in all these cases, if breathing has stopped. The hands should be placed on each side of the end of the rib cage, which should be pressed and allowed to expand in time with one's own breathing. In the case of a very small dog mouth to mouth respiration can be tried. The whole of the dog's mouth and nostrils must be covered if this is to succeed.

153

GLOSSARY

Allrounder—a judge authorized by the AKC to judge all breeds.

Anal glands—two, marble-sized glands located on either side of the anus which may excrete a thick, evil-smelling substance.

Apron—the long hair below the neck and on the chest of long-haired breeds. Also known as the frill.

Belton—the name given to the blue-and-white, or lemon-and-white flecking on the coats of English Setters.

Bench—a benched show is where dogs are displayed on platforms when not actually in the ring being judged.

B.O.B.—Best of Breed, the animal judged best of that particular breed at a show.

B.O.S.—Best Opposite Sex, the animal judged best of the opposite sex to the B.O.B.

B.I.S.—Best In Show, the animal judged best of all breeds at a show.

Brace—two dogs of the same breed but not necessarily the same sex. A well-matched brace will have the same color and markings.

Breeding Terms—a leasing out of a bitch by the owner to someone else for the purpose of breeding from her.

Brood—a bitch kept for breeding rather than for show.

Butterfly nose—a parti-colored nose.

Canker—a common term covering a multitude of ear troubles.

Catalogue—a list of dogs entered at a show, giving name, ownership, parentage, age and so on.

Cat foot—round, compact foot, with arched toes.

C.D.—Companion Dog, a title awarded to dogs that have attained certain minimum scores in licensed obedience trials (U.S.A.) or a Working Trials C.D. Stake (Great Britain).

Ch.—Champion, a title awarded to a dog that has defeated a specified number of dogs in specified competitions at a series of shows (U.S.A.) or a winner of three Challenge Certificates under three different judges (Great Britain).

Challenge Certificate—an award for the best exhibit in each sex in a breed at a Championship Show. Often referred to as a C.C. (Great Britain).

Championship Show—one to which the Kennel Club grants C.C.'s (Great Britain).

Cow hocks—hocks that turn inward toward each other.

Cryptorchid—an adult male whose one or both testicles are abnormally retained in the abdominal cavity.

Dew Claw—a functionless toe found as a rudimentary claw on the lower inside portion of a dog's leg. Often removed in early puppyhood though some breeds retain them.

Exemption Show—a show where permission has been granted by the K.C. for unregistered dogs to be exhibited (Great Britain).

Feathering—the long fringes of hair found on the legs, ears, tail and body of some breeds.

F.T.Ch.—Field Trial Champion, a title won by a gundog or Hound as a result of competition at Field Trials.

Gazehound—a generic name for all the hounds that hunt by sight. Also known as Windhounds or Sighthounds.

Hare foot—a long, narrow foot.

Harlequin—the patched coloring of some Great Danes.

Haw—the inner or third eyelid, unusually prominent in some breeds.

H.D.—Hip Dysplasia, a deformity of the hip joint.

Height—measured in dogs from the top of the withers to the ground.

Hock—the joint of the hind legs equivalent to the ankle joint in man.

Int. Ch.—International Champion, a dog that has won the title in more than one country.

Kennel Name—a distinguishing name granted to breeders for their exclusive use when registering their dogs.

Landseer—the black-and-white coloration of some Newfoundlands.

Limited Show—one limited in some way in the number of exhibitors (Great Britain).

Loin—region between the last rib and the hindquarters.

Mask—dark shading on the muzzle of some breeds.

Matron—a bitch that has had a litter.

Merle—a bluish-gray color flecked with black.

Monorchid—a unilateral cryptorchid.

Ob. Ch.—Obedience Champion, a dog that has won three Test C classes at Obedience Championship Shows (Great Britain).

Occiput—the bone at the upper back of the skull.

Open Show—one open to all comers (Great Britain).

Outcross—the mating of unrelated animals of the same breed.

Overshot—the front teeth of the upper jaw projecting some way over those in the lower jaw when the mouth is closed.

Pastern—the lower section of the leg between the knee and the foot.

P.D.—Police Dog, a title won by a dog that has attained certain minimum scores in P.D. tests (Great Britain).

P.R.A.—Progressive Retinal Atrophy, an inherited eye condition resulting in blindness in the adult animal.

Quick—part of the nail containing blood vessels and nerves.

Registration—the recording of a dog's name, parentage and ownership and assignment of a number with the appropriate K.C. on payment of a fee.

Roan—a mixture of colored hairs with white.

Sable—a sprinkling of black hairs over an under-lying lighter color.

Sanction Show—a show limited to members of the promoting club. The classification excludes dogs that have won a C.C. (Great Britain).

Schedule—a list of classes for a forthcoming show sent with the entry form to intending exhibitors.

Sh. Ch.—Show Champion, a title held by a gundog which has gained three C.C.'s but has not got the necessary qualifying certificate at a Field Trial for full Championship status (Great Britain).

Spay—removing the ovaries of a bitch to prevent conception.

Specialist—a judge interested in only one or a few breeds.

Stifle—the joint of the hind leg corresponding to a man's knee.

Stop—the indentation of the bone between the eyes.

Stud dog—the male animal used for breeding purposes.

T.A.F.—Transfer Applied For, these letters appear in show catalogues after the name of a dog whose ownership is in the process of being transferred (Great Britain).

T.D.—Tracking Dog, a title won by a dog that has attained certain minimum scores in tracking tests (U.S.A.), or open T.D. Stakes at Working Trials (Great Britain).

Team—more than two dogs of the same breed matched as to color and markings.

Throwback—a dog resembling some remote ancestor.

Transfer—the recording of a change of ownership with the appropriate K.C. on payment of a fee.

U.D.—Utility Dog, a title won by a dog which has attained certain minimum scores in a Utility class (U.S.A.) or a U.D. Stake at Working Trials (Great Britain).

Undershot—where the lower incisors project some way beyond the upper incisors when the mouth is closed.

Wall eye—a white or china blue eye.

Winners—awards given at American dog shows to the best dog and the best bitch competing in regular classes.

Withers—the highest point of the shoulder blades.

Wrinkle—the loose folds of skin on the forehead and sides of the muzzle in some breeds.

W.D.—Working Dog, a title won by a dog that has attained certain minimum scores in Working Trials (Great Britain).

W.T.Ch.—Working Trials Champion, a title given to a dog that has won two Ch. Working Trial Stakes (whether W.D., P.D. or T.D.) with more than a certain minimum score (Great Britain).

INDEX

Page numbers in bold type
refer to illustrations

Aggression 35, 38, 39
Agility tests **62, 63,** 64-65
American Utility tests 66, 70
Artificial insemination 109
Artificial respiration 153, **153**

Bath 22, **80,** 88-89, 92, 95
Barking 50, 52
Bed 10, 11, 25, **127,** 126-127
Behavior
    before rest **42,** 43
    instinctive 34-35
    juvenile 41, **41**
    sexual 36
    under stress 42
Benched show **74,** 81
Bitch 6, 10, **10,** 16, 34, 36, **37,** 38, 43, **43,** 96-97, 99, 106-111, **108**
Body sensitivity 31-32
Breeding 96-121
Brush 22, **22,** 83, 85, 90-92, 94, 95

Car-sickness 52-53
Chains **48, 81**
Challenge Certificates 78 **154**
Clippers **22,** 24, 86, 92-93
Coat 83-95
Collar 48, **48,** 81
Color breeding **101,** 103
Comb 22, **22,** 90, 92
Commands 55, 56-57
Cropping 114, **114**
Cryptorchidism 105

Deodorant 23, 43, 108
Dew-claws 112, **113**
Diet 13, 19-21, 91, 126, 132-133, 148
Distemper 16, 150, 152
Docking 113, **113**
Dog coat **21,** 25, 148
Dog whistle 30
Dumb-bell 58-59

Ears 88, 138-139, **138,** 148
English Saddle Clip 93
Entropion **104,** 105, 139, 148
Estrus cycle 106-107
Exercise 15, 21, 24, **79,** 80
Exercises
    distant control 60, 70-71
    'Down-stay' 57
    heelwork 56, **56,** 57
    recall 57, **57,** 58
    retrieve 58-59, 66, **67** 70-73

scent discrimination **58,** 59, **59**
'Seek back' 70-71, **70,** 73
'Send away' 60
'Stand for examination' 66-67, **66,** 83
'Stand-stay' 57, 58, 67
Eyes 28–30, 81, 88, 94, 105, 113, **138,** 139, 147, 148

Feeding bench **18**
Fights 40
Flea 23, **23**
Food intake
    ratio **20**
    of puppy 13, 17

Grooming 22–24, 83–95, **83**
Grooming table 84
Guard dog 53, **53**
Guide dog **31,** 32, 47, 109
Gun dog 60

Hardpad 150
Harness 72
Health 147-153
Hepatitis 16, 150-152
Hip joint 144-145, **144, 145**
Hip Dysplasia 104, **105**
Hound glove 22, **22,** 83, **83**
Hound trail 72
House training 14-15

Inbreeding 100
Inheritance 101, 102-105, **102, 103**
Inoculations 7, 16, 119, 151

Jumping *see* Agility tests
Jumping up 48, **49**

Kennel 91, 96-97, 106 122-131, **122, 123**
    construction 123-126
    design 122
    heating 126-127, **126**
    isolation 128-129
    ready-made **124**
    service area 130-131, **130**
    waste disposal 128, **128**
    whelping 129-130
Kennel Clubs 8, 55, 62, 76-78, 105

Lameness 150
Lead training **14,** 15, 48, 56-57

Leptospiral infections 16 150-152
Line-breeding 100, **100**
Litter 96-97, **96,** 106-107 109, 112-113, **112**
Longevity 27
Louse **23**

Mating 120, **120,** 121
Meat 13, 19-21
Mineral supplements 13 20-21, 110, 115, 133
Movement 140-143

Nail clippers 19, **23,** 24
Nails 19, 24, 81
Nose 32-33

Obedience Competition **54,** 55, 60-61, 62, 66, **66** 77
Old dog 24-27
Olfactory membrane 32

Patella Luxation 104
Pedigreed animal 4, 5, 77, 98-99
Police dog 47, 60, 64, **6**
Poodle clipping 92-93
Posture
    aggressive 39, **39, 41**
    nervous **38,** 39
    submissive 38-39, **38**
Praise 47, 50-51, 55, 73
Pregnancy 110
Progressive Retinal Atrophy 105
Pro-estrus period 36
Pug 29
Puppies 10-17, **10, 12, 1** **17,** 96-98, 111-119
    bedding 11
    birth of 110-113, **110** **111**
    carrying 10, **11**
    collection 12
    development 17
    feeding 13, 118-119
    hand rearing 118-11 **118**
    house traing 14
    lead training **14**
    selling 116
    showing 79
    traveling box 116-1 **117**
    weaning 114-115
    worming 114
Puppy Clip 93

Rabies 16

Registration certificate 8, 99, 116
Regurgitation 43, **43**
Rejuvenating drug 26
Road accidents 152
Roundworms 16-17, **16** 114

Saliva 33
Scent **68**, 69, **69**, marking 34-35, **35**
Scolding 50-51
Sense of smell 32, 68-73
Sexual organs **106**
Shampoo 88
Shelter 19, **19**
Shows 74-95
Skeleton 134, **134**
Skull 136-137, **136**, **137**

Slip collar 48, 56
Spaying 109
Scratching 149, **149**
Stripping 86-87
Stud dog 106, 109, 120-121

Tail **142**, 143, **143**
Tapeworms **16**
Teeth 80-81, **81**, 137
Temperament 8, 98
Terriers **26**, 27, 85-87, **85** **86**, **87**, **94**, 95, **95**, 114, 143
Tidbits 47
Toy dogs 18, 27, 82, 94, 105, 123
Toys **15**
Tracking **6**, 33, 68-73

Training
  car travel 52, **52**
  classes 55
  domestic 47
  puppy 44-50
  specialized 54-73
  to come 50, **50**
  see Exercises
Trimming 23, 84, 86-87, 89

Urination 14-15, 34, 108

Vitamin supplements 13, 20-21, 25, 110, 115, 133

Wire rake **22**
Working dogs 76
Working Trials 60, 62, 64 71, 77

Wendy Boorer started showing dogs at 14
and now runs a highly successful show-
kennel. Although she has only recently
started writing, Ms. Boorer already has several dog books to her credit.